girl
meets
girl

girl
meets
girl

a dating survival guide
diana cage

alyson books
NEW YORK

© 2007 by diana cage. all rights reserved.

manufactured in the united states of america

this trade paperback original is published by
alyson books, p.o. box 1253, old chelsea station,
new york, new york 10113-1251

distribution in the united kingdom by
turnaround publisher services ltd.,
unit 3, olympia trading estate, coburg road, wood green,
london n22 6tz united kingdom

first edition: january 2007

07 08 09 10 a 10 9 8 7 6 5 4 3 2 1

isbn 10 15583-989-4
isbn 13 978-1-55583-989-5

an application for library of congress cataloging-in-publication data
has been filed

book design by victor mingovits

contents

introduction: dating doesn't have to be difficult

dating doesn't have to be difficult

DATING DOESN'T HAVE to suck. Dating can even be fun if you do it right. All you need is a little guidance, a few rules to follow, and some common dating sense. And that's where this book comes in.

The idea for this book came out of many long phone conversations with my previous editor at Alyson books, Angela Brown. I was the editor of *On Our Backs* magazine and she was the editor-in-chief at Alyson, and we'd forged a friendship while working together on the *On Our Backs Guide to Lesbian Sex*. She was dating various people in Los Angeles. I was in San Francisco and my dating life was so frenzied it looked like a game of whack-a-mole. Every Monday morning we'd get to our respective offices and call each other up and discuss our weekend escapades. My dating tales and stories about the social scene in San Francisco and the other big cities I traveled to always astounded her. As the editor of the biggest LGBT publishing house, Angela was smart enough to spot trends in queer culture. She was registering the fact that the dating world was changing and she asked me to write a guidebook. Since she was the boss, I wrote up an outline and handed it over.

She had a point. There was nothing out there for queer chicks dating other queers that didn't just replay some of the old lesbionic jokes and clichés. Not that there's anything wrong with those old school ideas, it's just that they didn't apply to what I saw going on around me. The women I knew wanted to date but they weren't ready to nest. They were working on their careers, or maybe were in school, and they wanted to have a good time while they figured their lives out. They wanted to enjoy being queer and were making up their own rules as they went along.

I had a pretty unique vantage point because by the time I really got down to writing this book I had left *On Our Backs* magazine, moved to New York and started working with *Velvetpark* magazine, the New York–based culture, art, and activism magazine for dykes. We were touring around hitting all the big gay gigs in the country and I got to talk to dykes everywhere about sex, dating, and relationships.

the new queer frontier

THE ONE THING that kept ringing true regardless of what state we were in was that there was a whole new nation of queer chicks out there trying to rewrite all the old rules. Much like feminism we'd entered a new wave of lesbianism. Even the term *lesbian* was being met with suspicion. It was too loaded and it's meaning had become obscured by the politics of who qualified as a lesbian and who didn't.

The population that was actively dating wasn't too worried about pronouns; they got the concept that gender and biology aren't necessarily related. They were trying to bring dating back, with roles and protocol and actual dates. Butch-femme was everywhere, but it was a postmodern kind of butch-femme where either role could be anything and everything and you could no longer make assumptions about someone based on the way they dressed. The dykes I met were over labels and identity politics. They loved their trans sisters, and were working their asses off to make up for the fact that transwomen have often felt excluded from the lesbian community. In fact, what they were doing was deconstructing the lesbian community and rebuilding it from the ground up to suit the way they wanted to live and fall in love.

I drafted this book with that info in mind. I included all the information I'd learned while traveling around. I talked to friends and people I was involved with. And I wrote down everything anyone told me and tried to fill this book with information that would speak to what I saw as my community.

language and labels

WHEN I GOT the first draft of the book back from my editor her queries were all about my use of language and labels. Some of our conversations were downright hilarious, like the time she told me to use the word "dildo" instead of "cock." She patiently explained to me—like I was from another planet—that not all dykes like to think of their dildo as a cock. I was skeptical. "Are you sure?" I said. I mean even the high femmes I know call it that. So I started asking around and found there were so many names for the thing I'd be better off just picking something and sticking with it. It came down to "cock" or "special friend" and I went with cock. I like to think we've degendered that word at this point.

It's difficult to talk about the experiences of queer women in a language that doesn't recognize our existence. I realize it's a radical concept, but it's just as easy to change the meaning of language as it is to create new language. I like to think we can de-male certain terms by bringing them into the vernacular of queer female experience. If we use them loudly enough their meaning will mutate.

As soon as we settled the dildo question we started going back and forth about terms for masculine-identified dykes. *Butch* is loaded and doesn't always apply, *boy* is too limiting. *Boi* is a good one but also loaded, and *Queer* is gender neutral. These things aren't a problem to navigate in our private lives but in a book they can be a little sticky. In the interest of making the text readable we need to use a label. But there are so many and they all mean different things to different people. I don't want to assign labels, but I did need to shorthand gender differences. In the end, I went with the way that these labels get used in the community I come from and that is, for the most part, interchangeably. It doesn't really matter what you call yourself or your girlfriend. The information still applies.

For the record, I fell hard for someone while I was writing this thing. So I feel like it might have some good mojo in it. I swear I was just skipping along doing my own thing, dating different people here and there and enjoying myself when *Bam!* Someone cute got in my way and the next thing you know little hearts were popping out of my eyes and I had to change my relationship status on Myspace.com.

I hope that you meet someone too, if that is your ultimate goal. And I also hope that this book helps you keep your sense of humor about dating and relationships. We're all in the same boat, we're all dating each other, and we're all queer. Sometimes it gets complicated, but most of the time it's fun. And I think it's important to point out the fun at least as often as we point out the drama. Go forth and date.

part one

the dating game

CHAPTER 1

back to basics

AS FAR AS I can tell, these days everyone wants a lesbian to call their own. Even straight girls. The minute they get sick of their boyfriends they start wishing they could date their best friend. And occasionally they do. And sometimes it even works.

Dykes are so cool we made those stupid trucker hats chic. We popularized faux-hawks. Um, hello. We brought back mullets? I realize some of us never really stopped wearing them—and even now wear them sans irony—but that just goes to show how iconoclastic our community is.

And what about sex? Dykes are the new gay men. The last big party I went to ended with all the dykes getting into one bed, and the gay guys cleaning up the empty bottles and sweeping the floor before heading home.

I don't know if you've noticed but straight people are strapping it on all over the place these days. Two major dyke-friendly sex-toy retailers, Babeland and Good Vibrations, claim straight couples account for a good portion of their strap-on sales, and the *Bend Over Boyfriend* instructional videos were made by a dyke video company. Add to that the fact that all the sensitive metrosexual guys want to get really good at eating pussy. A few years ago there was an article in *Details* magazine, the bible of the sensitive, gay-friendly metrosexual, about how to go downtown. The writer flew all the way out to San Francisco, home of the queerest of queers, to interview a butch lesbian about rug-munching.

Come on, kids, just admit you think being a big homo is sexy. Everyone's doing it. Throw a drink and you'll probably hit someone about to go for a Sapphic spin.

I blame *The L Word*.

So, what's a gal to do with all this extra estrogen floating around?

Well, in the immortal words of my dearest friend, Jess, when girls come out, you have to date them to make sure they stay gay.

Recruit them, I say. Especially if they're cute.

The important thing to remember is that the odds are in your favor if you're looking for the girl of your dreams (or for a night). But before you get started, you're going to need deprogramming. How you can you get the girl if you're crippled by lame lesbian stereotypes, poor self-esteem, bedroom-performance anxiety, lack of mojo—or, worst of all, you're so far in the closet you're practically in Narnia?

Read on, cupcake. I'm going to show you how to become the Don Juan of Dyke Dating.

how to tell if you need this book

The last date you went on ended with:

a. A good-night kiss
b. An STD
c. A live-in girlfriend
d. I haven't had a date since they canceled Melrose Place

The best way to get a date with a girl is:

a. Say "I'd like to take you on a date"
b. Call her obsessively and hang up without leaving a message
c. Act like you hate her and make out with other girls when she's around
d. Tell her your boyfriend wants to watch the two of you have sex

A good place to meet available women is:

a. Queer film festivals
b. Frat parties (drunk girls are easy)
c. Prison
d. Star Trek conventions

KEY: If you answered anything but A to the above questions, then you'd better read on, honey.

lesbian relationship myths destroyed

OK, SOMETIMES IT'S hard work being a dyke. If you are good at it you have to deal with bullshit on all sides. Straight guys find you either threatening or hot. Straight girls find you titillating or scary. The media ignores you (or you wish they would). Gay men ignore you. Your only role models are sports stars and Melissa Etheridge, and if you aren't into either of those things, you're fucked.

There are so many tired stereotypes about lesbians, sex and relationships that we could fill a whole chapter with them, but most hearken back to the Beebo Brinker days when there were few options other than to lurk in dark bars by night and live in the closet by day.

Budding baby lesbians come out in elementary school these days. OK, maybe not everywhere, but in some places. Queer and questioning kids have no problem seeing images of same-sex sexuality on TV and not just on *Cops*. While it's still not completely positive one hundred percent of the time, gone are the days of Mercedes McCambridge playing a closeted bulldagger or of lusting after Jo from *The Facts of Life* but not really knowing why. When you are a budding baby homo it's pretty easy to recognize the queer characters on TV. Even if they aren't openly gay, there's something there that speaks to us. Sometimes it's an artistic talent, or an outsider stance. Or they could have a fey or butch way of carrying themselves. Whatever it is, we know when someone is purposefully acting *different*. And these days it's becoming a little easier to read that difference as something attractive. I love seeing positive representations of queers in art, film, and literature. The more we are reflected in a positive way the less internal turmoil we experience about the way we fall in love.

More and more our recognition of ourselves and other people as queer takes place early enough to prevent a lot of the feelings of isolation that many of us used to experience as wee gay babes. That means we're a healthier, more self-aware nation of queers. A healthier nation of queers that wants to date, get laid, fall in love, and eventually settle down, move to Canada, and get gay-married to each other. Or some combination thereof.

myth #1: lesbians skip dating and go straight to living together (also known as the u-haul syndrome)

This is that tired old belief that when two girls date they immediately move in together. Sure, it happens. But it happens with straight people and gay men, too. It's not particular to lesbians. Sometimes people just fall in love right away. Sometimes people are needy and lonely, and they meet someone else who is also needy and lonely, and they click and settle down immediately. Sometimes people move in together out of convenience and pragmatism. But whatever the reason, the lesbian version of this is not as common as all the jokes would have you believe.

Queer women date each other without immediately jumping into relationships. Dykes have sex, even casual sex, even (gasp!) anonymous sex. Dykes want to get to know someone before they move in together; they may want to eventually settle down and have a bunch of babies or a Golden Retriever or maybe just a flat-screen TV. But I've never met anyone who seriously wanted to move right in with the first gal who came along. What kind of crazy behavior is that? It goes without saying you should get to know someone a bit before you make promises and lifelong commitments. As for bringing the U-Haul on the second date? If you do spot this type, run.

Many of us aren't even interested in settling down at all. There are women of all ages who simply want to go through life having a series of love affairs. These women value their independence and find that having lovers and friends suits them more than having a serious partner.

myth #2: lesbians don't have a lot of sex (also known as lesbian bed-death syndrome).

You may have noticed that women are widely considered to be less sexual than men. Apparently lesbians are a lot like giant pandas and are way more into cuddling than getting it on. Or at least that's what the media tells us. But nothing could be further from the truth. I really think that this myth is something propogated by our patriarchal society. No one wants to think about chicks screwing each other all the time when there's no penis in sight. It just makes penises seem kind of obsolete. And that makes the people that run the world kind of uncomfortable. The real truth is dykes have more sex than you can imagine. Dykes are the ones throwing the sex parties, teaching the sexy workshops, having multiple lovers, opening sex-toy stores, reading and writing erotica, and educating themselves and each other about sex. Lesbian relationships are hot, sexy, and multi-orgasmic.

Dating is as much about having sex as it is about looking for a relationship. And if I had my way this book would be called *The Queer Girl's Guide to Getting Laid a Lot*. So I've thrown plenty of advice in that direction. Use it wisely.

myth #3: bi girls are just experimenting and will leave you for a man (also known as the kissing jessica stein syndrome)

In the nineties when femmes were called lipstick lesbians and it was all the rage to experiment with girl-on-girl love, chicks who had been queer all their lives resented these tourists in the lesbian nation for what they saw as their straight privilege. Bi-curious, bisexual, or otherwise ladies weren't seen as "real" lesbians. They were just playing around with the swinging Sapphic set, looking for a little fun before going back to straightville armed with new sexual skills and trailing broken hearts in their wake.

But that's an outdated way of thinking, propagated by fear, internalized homophobia, and having grown up in a society that's so sexually repressed everyone had to gather into factions just so they'd have backup in case of attack.

Girls who don't necessarily identify as dykes are dating each other and enjoying it. In our post-label, polyamorous, open-minded, sex-positive world, female-bodied individuals regardless of their sexual identity are happily hooking up. Any combo meal you can think up is probably happening at the gay bar down the street, so why worry about what we're calling it anymore?

Lesbian + bi girl + lesbian + transguy + butch lesbian + straight girl + straight girl + bi dyke + boi + femme lesbian + bulldagger + bi curious + transwoman + polygirl + queer + boi + womyn + grrl + soft butch + androdyke + aggressive + high femme + execudyke + transgirl + stud + bi boi+ whatever + dyke + gay boy + lipstick lesbian + straight girl

Historically dykes have policed the boundaries of dyke sexuality by shunning girls who might want to date another woman but not throw out their straight friends and ex-boyfriends. This kind of biphobia exists because, as marginalized queer women, we don't have much power in greater society. But we feel a sense of power when we throw around the idea that you have to qualify in order to be a lesbian. By deciding what is and what isn't lesbian we keep our communities and our culture intact.

The insularity that women who date other women build around themselves serves to protect us in a society that, let's face it, is pretty much controlled by dudes. A lesbian relationship is at a disadvantage in a patriarchy. Straight women are second-class citizens just like we are, but they have a male partner. And just the virtue of having a male partner gives them a security in a society rife with misogyny and power imbalances. In order to counteract this, women dating other women often choose to keep not only their relationships private but their lives out of the mainstream. Our relationships are intense; the sex we have is intense. And we are careful about who we let have this information. No one wants to risk letting in people who might spoil the whole game.

Our self-protective actions stem from an honest desire to make our lives safer. But it's an outmoded way of functioning that is changing. Sure, you might bump into a woman who was once burned by a bi girl and doesn't want to date you, but then she's not right for you. Or maybe it's time for you to open up your idea of what queer is, so you can meet the right person. Queer women will find power in numbers, in solidarity, in visibility. Not in hiding away so no one can see us.

So, I say if they want to eat pussy, let 'em! Build up the lesbian nation. Go down on a bi-curious girl today.

myth #4: one of you has to be the girl, and the other has to be the boy. (otherwise known as the "who wears the strap-on" syndrome)

Assigning boy or girl labels to certain traits is a pretty common pitfall in our society. And dating chicks doesn't exactly free you from it. In fact, once you have two women together it actually gets a little more confusing. We were all raised to think in gender roles. You know the dumb drill: boys play with GI Joe; girls play with Barbie. Boys play football; girls take ballet. So even if you really do realize that sort of thinking is stunted, it's still hard to avoid its effects. And even if you work hard to keep it from affecting you, you will still run into people who are caught up in it. And you might even end up going out with them.

What this means to your dating life is that some traits particular to sex and relationships, such as who is the aggressor in bed, who does the asking out on dates, or who pays for dinner, get put in the masculine category. And if you don't think of yourself as masculine you may not feel comfortable taking them on. Maybe you are so girly that you don't know how to do any of those things and you are just lying around with your legs open hoping someone will trip and fall between them. If that's the case, it's going to be a lot harder for you to get what you want. So throw all that stuff about boy/girl, masculine/feminine out and then relearn it in a queer context. It's perfectly OK to be aggressive and confident. It doesn't make you a boy; it makes you hot.

Sure, there are butch-femme queer couples who have masculine and feminine gender roles, but that doesn't mean one person is the "boy." Besides, not all girls who date girls fall into butch-femme roles and even those who do aren't having a boy-girl relationship.

If you are a queer woman involved with a transman then, yes, there's a boy involved. But he doesn't have to be the aggressor, the top, or the person who pays. He doesn't have to do anything traditionally masculine unless you both agree that traditional roles are hot to you. And if that's the case, you can still divvy them up any way you see fit. There is no law in lesbo land.

There are plenty of "boys" in the land of gay dating. They go by many names depending on what community they are part of. Sometimes chicks who enjoy taking on a more aggressive role are "butch," sometimes they are "aggressives," sometimes they are "studs," "bois," "boys," "transmen," "trannyboys," "dykes," "tops," "stone," and many other names. If you want to date someone who enjoys taking on a typically masculine role, that person won't be hard to find. But if you are a chick who digs on another chick, put your little head to rest over gender roles. Just give your long hair a toss, put on some lipstick, and go for it.

find your inner player

THE FIRST STEP to enjoying this weird game called dating is to locate your inner player. It's not as bad as it sounds. I'm not condoning misogyny, heart breaking, chick stealing, or excessive LL Cool J listening. I'm just saying it's OK to want to hook up here and there and not think you need to shack up with every hottie you meet. It's OK, more than OK—it's a good thing—to want to be sexual, to explore your sexuality, to feel sexy and flirt and turn people on.

The reason I encourage women to seek out this part of themselves is that most of us are raised to think desire is something we should suppress. Regardless of our gender very few of us escape internalizing the good girl/bad girl dichotomy that exists all over our society. And dating a lot, sleeping with more than one person, and embracing our need for sex usually falls into that "bad girl" category.

You can deal with this in several ways. One way women have tried to conquer this issue is by embracing the bad girl stereotype and claiming it as their own. Like we have reclaimed the word "dyke," we can reclaim the word "slut." Lots of women use "slut" as shorthand for describing a sex-positive, self-possessed, happily unattached, or polyamorous person.

Another way to move past the idea that wanting to meet new people for sex and dating is a "bad girl" trait is to rewrite the rules.

The rules were all written a long time ago. And they probably don't really work for you. More than that, they favor heteros. Straight folks have been setting the standard for a while now. And according to the majority of the hetero world, we're all supposed to fall in love with one person, have a traditional marriage, move to the suburbs, buy a three-bedroom house, and start making babies ASAP. Then we are supposed to work soul-sucking jobs, lose interest in our spouse, sleep with the next-door neighbor, and get a messy divorce. I'm just calling it like I see it.

Heterosexism is slightly different from homophobia in that rather than seeing homosexuality as just plain wrong, it simply sees heterosexuality as the default, or perhaps as the right way to act. And anything outside of heterosex is weird or other or something to be avoided. Not falling into the trap of unquestioningly following heterosexist paradigms is a practice unto itself. But it's one worth attempting. Let go of unnecessary baggage and rewrite rules in a useful way.

self-esteem: the most important meal of the day

HOW IS YOUR self-esteem? Let's have a little talk about it, shall we? Sit down over here on my lap. I'm going to let you in on a secret. No one likes people who don't like themselves. It's just not attractive. In fact, it's repelling. Come on. Go up to the mirror and give yourself a little Stuart Smalley ego check-in: "I'm good enough, I'm smart enough, and gosh darn it, people like me."

Self-esteem is more complicated when you are queer because even if you were raised to think highly of yourself, you are trying to date and fall in love in a way that is pretty much considered weird if not downright wrong by most of the powerful people in our society.

Our self-esteem affects every facet of our existence. It affects what jobs we choose to pursue, it affects our romantic lives, it affects how we dress, it affects how we treat ourselves and other people.

i like myself

When we have high self-esteem, it's likely that we have received mostly positive messages about ourselves throughout our lives. And because we were never taught to think of ourselves as anything but fantastic we naturally avoid situations in which we might get taken advantage of. People with high self-esteem are more likely to pursue healthy relationships, and to have sex because they want to have sex and not because they are trying to get attention or manipulate someone. High self-esteem folks take care of themselves, practice good boundaries, and generally live happy lives.

i'm not so sure about myself

Low-self esteem usually comes from receiving negative messages about ourselves, often in early childhood. Sometimes it's from our families. Sometimes it happens because we were big gay homos at an early age and the people around us in school didn't understand why we acted and looked different from them. We carry that stuff around with us all throughout our lives and it affects the way we are in the world. When we have low self-esteem, we worry people won't like us and often allow ourselves to fall into unhealthy situations in order to get attention, affection, or approval. Low self-esteem can mean an individual won't pursue relationships at all, or will pursue relationships obsessively, constantly looking for approval and affection from anyone who will pay attention to them.

Regardless of whether you are a big gay homo or someone just curious about a same-sex experience, you were raised in a society that believes queer desire is wrong. And in order to have healthy relationships we need to throw that information out and start fresh.

Even if you managed to escape childhood with positive feelings about sex and desire or learned to get over the negative messages you received, it's likely you will at some point come in contact with other queer women who haven't managed that.

So first and foremost you should look at your own self-esteem. How do you feel about yourself? Do you like yourself? Do you feel like you are worthwhile and people want to spend time with you? Because if *you* don't think that about yourself, no one else will think it about you.

Approach this honestly. It's for your own good.

10 things another person would find attractive about you

1.
2.
3.
4.
5.
6.
7.
8.
9.
10.

How easy was it to come up with ten things? If it was easy for you, great! Keep this list handy and refer to it as necessary. Post it on the fridge.

If it wasn't easy, try and figure out some reasons that might be the case. Did you receive a lot of negative messages from your parents or other authority figures? And if so, what can you do to turn those around? Awareness is the first step. Therapy is often the fastest route to rewiring the negative messages we've received. I recommend that everyone get therapy. It's an essential part of a healthy lifestyle, like going to the gym. But if you aren't interested in therapy or it's out of your reach financially or for some other reason, then work on turning those messages around on your own.

Try making another list: ten things that aren't very attractive about yourself. Now, really take a look at the list. Think over each thing you've written down. Do you really think no one will ever find you attractive because you have big feet? Once you look at your so-called flaws with a critical eye you will start to realize how silly they are. Are there things on your list that seem inescapable? We'll break down each item with a list of ways you can change that quality.

OK, yeah, the *Saturday Night Live* skit with Stuart Smalley giving himself positive affirmation in the mirror is meant to be stupid satire. But that doesn't mean that creating positive messages out of negative ones doesn't work. Reminding yourself on a regular basis that you are attractive and worthwhile can help you start believing it about yourself. Being out in the dating world means occasionally facing rejection. And if your self-esteem is intact, that rejection won't register as much more than a tiny blip on your radar. Try and remind yourself as often as you can that you are desirable, but that doesn't mean that every person will desire you. And that's fine. Who cares? If they don't like you, screw them. There's probably something wrong with them anyway.

repeat after me: "i have a beautiful body"

YOU HAVE A beautiful body. I don't care if you are butch or femme or neither or other or in between. I don't care if you have a big butt, no butt, small tits, or a big belly. Big butts are sexy. Small butts are sexy. Anything that's on a chick is sexy. You know why? Because chicks are sexy. And chicks who love their bodies are the sexiest.

The way you look is just fine. We all get so hung up on comparing ourselves to people we believe to be beautiful and then quantifying the ways in which we are not like those beautiful people that it's a wonder anyone has time to get laid.

I hate the way women I find stunning torture themselves over the teeny-tiniest little thing. We don't see ourselves the way others see us. We concentrate on our flaws and see ourselves as a series of parts rather than as a whole person. Anyone is gorgeous when they love themselves.

Queer standards of beauty are different from the standards of beauty set by mainstream society. That's one of the amazing things about being queer: getting to set up your own rules. Not having many role models has a positive aspect in that we also don't have really well-established and unattainable standards for attractiveness. But unfortunately the standards set by the rest of the world still affect us. And when we don't love ourselves and our bodies, we walk around with a physical language that says, "Stay away!" The most imperfect person will get lots of attention if she carries herself with confidence. And the most beautiful creature will turn people off if she feels ugly.

The fastest way to ruin your sex life, whether in a relationship or a fling, is to stop feeling as if you are sexy.

so, how do i feel sexy?

Well, duckling, I'm going to tell you. Being sexy is completely unrelated to being perfect, skinny, feminine, pretty, and any of the other adjectives you'd apply to Barbie. Being sexy is about projecting sex appeal. And sex appeal comes in a whole slew of

10 ways to get your sexy mojo going

1. Smile at a cute stranger, but don't stare or you'll look loony.
2. Rent *Showgirls* and practice talking like Cristal Connors: Call everyone Darlin'.
3. Find a nontraditionally beautiful role model: Queen Latifah is big and beautiful.
4. Rent any Annie Sprinkle video, or read her book *Dr. Sprinkle's Spectacular Sex.*
5. Check out some hot dyke photography. I recommend Phyllis Christopher's Photo DVD *Sextrospective: A Decade with San Francisco's Sexiest Lesbians,* available online at www.thesexystuff.com.
6. Place a Craigslist ad; even just flipping through the responses will wake up your inner diva.
7. Change something about yourself—hair, clothes— just try a new look.
8. Go to a sex party.
9. Learn to salsa, then bust out with your new moves at a queer club.
10. Attend a sex-ed workshop and learn a new skill.

forms.

Don't believe me? Think about this: When we see a packing butch, we think she's sexy. I don't care what gender you are: If you are a dyke, even a dyke in training, a packing butch dyke radiates sex appeal.

OK, so what is it about a packing butch that's sexy? She doesn't have to look like Marlon Brando in *Streetcar*. Hell, she can look like Marlon Brando in *The Island of Dr. Moreau*. It's not her physical appearance we're responding to—it's the idea that she's confident enough to project a readiness for sex, and cocky, so to speak, enough to wear her cock in public.

The same goes for a woman dressed in high heels and walking with confidence. We find her sexy because she's projecting her desire for sex. Carrying sex toys with you makes you sexy. Carrying safer-sex supplies indicates you are ready for sex and prepared to think about your partner's health and well-being, and that's sexy, too.

Smiling, laughing, being playful and flirtatious are all sexy. Speaking your mind makes you sexy. Being independent makes you sexy. Making eye contact makes you sexy. Knowing how to please a partner makes you hella sexy.

learn to work your assets

WANT TO FEEL more confident about your appearance? Figure out what you really look like, and accept yourself. Figure out what is specifically attractive about you, and learn to work your assets. If you are a more androgynous- or masculine-looking babe, don't hide that part of yourself with makeup or feminine trappings. Work that shit. Cut your hair. Display your gender with pride. Fly the freak flag. Embrace yourself and the ways you are different. They make you hot. Girls will be throwing their panties at you before you know it.

Are you a big girl? Big girls are ha-cha. The bigger the better, more to love, you know what I mean? Cities like San Francisco, Chicago, Boston, and New York are all filled with burlesque troops full of big, glorious, fabulous femmes of size. Get on the Internet and find one, then go out and buy some pasties and shake your tatas to your heart's content.

Not girly? Are you big and butch? Well, honey, play your cards right and femmes will be cat-fighting over you. Embrace your size. Show me a femme and I'll show you someone who is looking for a big bulldagger. All it takes is confidence. If you walk around hunched over and shy, hiding your body under mounds of clothes, no one will ever notice you. Go get yourself some nice-fitting 501s and a work shirt, and strut over to the local woman-loving-woman watering hole and see if you don't get lucky.

Got beautiful eyes? Enhance them, flirt with them, glance coyly at people with them. What about nice hands? Show them off. Are you tall? Wear heels and dress to enhance your Amazon stature. Are you boyish? Wear clothes that show off your slim hips and flat chest. Curvy and very feminine? Wear corsets and skirts. Dress in a way that flatters your body and don't follow trends that don't work for you.

I'm a short, curvy femme. I'm not perfect, and my body is definitely not skinny nor does it fit traditional mainstream standards of beauty. But people find me sexy. I rarely lack for lovers or attention. And while I wasn't always as comfortable in my skin as I am now, the reason I'm sexy is mostly because I've accepted my body the way it is. I dress to show off my curviness rather than hide it. I know I don't look like a Calvin Klein model and I never will. And that's OK. Over the years my various girlfriends have loved my tits, my ass, my lips, my smile, and the gap between my front teeth. And no one has ever said they hated my thighs, my round face, my soft shape, my thick legs, my strong arms or any of the other things *I've* hated about myself. The only person who even thought those parts of my body were ugly was me.

you can't date in the closet

YOU CANNOT—I REPEAT, *cannot*—have a successful dating experience if you are closeted in any way. I don't even care if you find someone in there with you. You can't just go deep into the closet and start hanging out with the White Queen and eating Turkish Delight.

OK, I know this is tough to hear, and I understand that if you are closeted it's for a good reason—your safety, emotional or physical—but, sweetie, this is for your own good.

There are many levels of outness and ways to express our queerness. But if you ultimately feel that there's something wrong with you for being a big gay homo, then you really aren't going to have a good time hanging out with other big gay homos since you probably think there's something wrong with them, too.

Besides, didn't you get the memo? All the quality people are gay now. Queerness is where it's at. Listen to me, sister: As queer women, we re-create things every day that the straight world simply takes for granted. Things like gender, fashion, love, relationships, art, community, social mores, values, and standards of beauty. Being queer requires an awareness of your surroundings that forces you to be a more sensitive, more complex individual.

Being in the closet means you don't have access to a large dating pool since you don't feel comfortable going to where the dykes are. Being closeted means you can't have fun on your dates because you are too worried about being spotted with another woman and pegged as a dyke. Being closeted means you can't be yourself. And when you can't be yourself with people, they feel uncomfortable and won't be able to get to know you.

I understand that it isn't as easy for all of us as I'd like to think. But I want you to think seriously about the ramifications of living with a secret about two of the things that make up the very core of our existence: sex and desire.

If being out in your community puts you in danger, you may seriously want to consider moving. Yes, moving seems hard, especially if you are rooted in a place because of your job or family. But we are talking about your whole life here. What's your quality of life like if you spend it with shame and fear? Seems pretty sucky, wouldn't you say? There are cities all over this country with big gay communities. You don't have to live in San Francisco or New York. Go find a nice cozy little gay Mecca in the Midwest. Do a little research. The world is slowly changing, but it might be a long while before it hits your town. In the meantime, there are dykes having lots of fun in towns and cities all over the country.

the five most lesbian-friendly cities according to gay.com

1. Brooklyn, New York
2. Los Angeles, California
3. San Francisco, California
4. Portland, Oregon
5. Phoenix, Arizona

sometimes it shows

Do people peg you as a dyke? Lucky you! I wish *I* got more props on the street. As a femme, I usually have to be on the arm of an obviously queer woman to get noticed by other queers.

Sometimes people know we are gay by simply reading our signifiers. We don't need to out ourselves. Most of the women I've been with have told me that they knew they were gay from the first moment they had an awareness of themselves. I've mostly been involved with butch women, and I sometimes wonder if their butchness is part of the reason they were aware of their desire so young. Being butch at a young age is a pretty good tip-off that you probably don't want to don the long white dress of love and vow to pop out a bunch of babies for some guy named Frank. Being obviously queer—whether it's because your gender presentation doesn't fit most people's expectations or because you've chosen clear signifiers—can mean that your daily life is more challenging than someone who blends in. Being out means dealing with homophobia and sexism. It means navigating people's preconceived notions about queer women and gender. Female masculinity definitely has its own set of challenges, but figuring out you're gay isn't often one of them.

sometimes it doesn't

Femmes and feminine girls however have their own set of issues around coming out. When we are feminine, all the messages that the media shows us about getting pursued by boys usually happen the way we'd expect them to. We don't always experience our own desire. Often the act of feeling desired clouds everything else. We do want to be desired, and since we are getting what we want, it takes a while to start to realize that we actually want to be desired by the head field-hockey player and not the captain of the football team.

My own awareness of my queerness came about much more slowly. And my experience is something that many femme bi girls, and all sorts of feminine people I know have shared. Because I was very feminine I had boyfriends and a dating life and all the things that straight girls have. I knew I liked fooling around with girls, but I just chalked it up to being open-minded and bi, and I didn't really think much about it. It wasn't until I moved to San Francisco and realized there were girls who liked fooling around with girls but who looked like boys that I realized how I wanted my love life to roll. There it was, the feeling I'd been looking for. Suddenly I was a big gay homo. But it wasn't until I discovered the yin-yang fit of butch-femme that I realized how I wanted to love and be loved.

and sometimes we don't know it ourselves

And then there are some of us who are neither particularly masculine nor particularly feminine. And we aren't attracted to folks who are particularly masculine or feminine. We aren't radiating a lot of sexual energy and desire and are maybe even viewed as sexless. This is really common when people are just coming out. If you knew you were queer and worried that it was wrong and didn't want people to find out, you may have put a lot of energy into repressing your sexuality and desire. Or perhaps you have had other things on your mind and it just never occurred to you to flaunt your sexiness. Well, if you are reading this book, then you're obviously on to something. You may have to do a little extra work to figure out how to flaunt your sexiness and set off the gaydar in that hottie behind the Starbucks counter. But once you've finished reading this book and you know what you want, all this attracting-chicks stuff will seem a whole lot easier.

so how do people come out?

THERE ARE LOTS of ways of letting people know about your desire to get jiggy with persons of your same sex. Some people choose to make it known to their families right away, in high school or junior high. Some people don't even realize it themselves until after they've raised a family and had a traditional marriage. If you aren't totally comfortable with the idea of letting everyone know, try telling a few people who you really trust first. It's perfectly OK to go through this process slowly, just as long as you go through it.

Alternatively, you can just start dating whomever the hell you like, and if people ask you questions about it, you can answer them honestly. That's *my* preferred method. Mostly because treating the idea of being gay as some sort of issue to be dealt with only reinforces heterosexuality as a norm. And as we all know, normalcy is subjective.

Regardless of how you choose to let the world know about your fabulous same-sex desires, keep in mind that the only person who needs to approve of your love life is you. Deal with your issues in therapy, a support group, with friends, or wherever you can find support. You don't want to let internalized homophobia cloud what might otherwise be a fabulous date.

signifiers, a.k.a. things that make gaydar go off

ONCE WE'VE COME out to our families and friends we still need to figure out ways to come out to people we want to get busy with. Queers do this in myriad ways, and it usually starts with a haircut. Girls figure out they want to attract other girls and they shave their heads. Boom! Instant dyke! This only works great if you like the look of yourself bald. Or if you are so new to being a lezzer that you haven't figured out anything past the point of wanting another girl. It's after you've been around a while and you start understanding dyke gender that different ways of presenting yourself and what you are attracted to make sense.

you look fabulous, darling

You know why queers love fashion? Because we use it to get laid. Just like gay men, dykes signify their sexuality, gender, desire, outlook, and all sorts of other things in the way they dress. There are ways to let other queers know you are a friend of Dorothy without resorting to rainbow gear.

Some of the signifiers that queers use to indicate their queerness and sexual orientation include things like work shirts, work boots, and mechanics jackets for that working-class butch look. Tailored button-down shirts and flat-front slacks say corporate dyke; pink sparkly things and feather boas say femme seeking butch. The sideways trucker cap–and–black-rimmed-glasses look was so prominent in San Francisco a few years back that people started referring to girls sporting it as Mission trolls—the Mission being a neighborhood that many dykes live in. If you were sporting the Mission troll look, everyone knew you were a dyke and could assume certain things about your tastes based on your aesthetic.

commonly seen lesbian looks

POWER LESBIAN: black-rimmed specs, Kenneth Cole pumps, Banana Republic wardrobe

SPORTY DYKE: nylon shorts, college sweatshirt, New Balance sneakers

BABY DYKE: Pride rings, awkward haircut

FEMME: cat-eye specs, Forever 21 wardrobe, red lipstick, eyeliner

HIGH FEMME: Forever 21 wardrobe, fuck-me pumps, bad attitude

BOI: Plaid short-sleeve shirt from Old Navy boy's section over vintage T-shirt

BUTCH: Button-down Oxford shirt, khakis, boxers

BULLDAGGER: wife beater, 501s, tattooed biceps

TWEENER: bobbed hair, Gap pants, pastel T-shirt

ANDRODYKE: Black pants, turtleneck sweater, slip-on shoes

Other ways we indicate we're queer include sporting Pride jewelry, dressing with an edge, looking unconventional, strutting around town with confidence, reading lesbian magazines, wearing masculine clothing, sporting studded belts, mullets, wallet chains, short fingernails, flannel, sensible shoes, T-shirts with gay slogans, bumper stickers, hanging out in gay places, drinking copious amounts of PBR, playing softball, riding motorcycles, talking about *The L Word*, having cats, being vegetarian, getting tattooed, getting pierced, belt buckles, Starbucks cards, small dogs, combat boots, Birkenstocks, reading Rita Mae Brown, becoming activists, being concerned for the environment.

queer pride faux pas

Being out and proud is great, but if you've got a rainbow sticker on your jeep, a flag on your front porch, an HRC sticker on your laptop, and a vanity plate that reads RGMNCHR, then I think you might be too gay. Reign it in a bit.

CHAPTER 2

ready, set, date

FIGURING OUT WHO you want to date is half the fun. Start fantasizing about your dream girl or boi: What does she look like? Who is she? Once you've pinpointed what you want you can start going after it. You also want to make sure you avoid some common dating pitfalls like dating before you are ready, getting involved with someone who's just had a break up, and getting so overwhelmed by choices you can't figure out who to go out with first.

your lady wish list

OK, YOU CAN'T date her if you don't know who she is or what she looks like. So you'll need to start figuring that out. I'm not saying you need to make an exact list of every trait your new lady friend needs to have. Because if you did that you'd be a freak and you'd end up spending an awful lot of Saturday nights watching *Buffy* on DVD. But getting a general idea of what you are looking for is going to help you start looking. Not only that but it will keep you from wasting your time with someone you ultimately are incompatible with. If you are always involved with people you feel lukewarm about, you'll be too busy to notice when someone really exciting comes along.

And knowing what you want is the first step to getting what you want.

make a list

Desire is a pretty abstract thing and you probably won't know what you really want until you meet a person that naturally fits you. But that doesn't mean you can't make a list of things you need. Just the process of writing it down will help you clarify it for yourself. And you will need a pretty clear idea of what you are looking for if you start looking to score a little strange out in the wide, wide world of the Internet. And you will, because everyone does.

Lists are very helpful. Lists can help you make decisions. I discovered this at seventeen when my friend Roxy suggested I make a list of pros and cons about having sex for the first time. There we were, sitting in a Carl's Jr. in San Diego eating fried zucchini and debating whether or not I should remain a virgin until I fell in love or simply get it on with someone I merely desired physically. We were very deep, of course. We read Kahil Gibran and talked a lot about love.

But we were also feminists and ready to own our sexuality. I read Germaine Greer's *The Female Eunuch* and I was all ready to tell whoever I was about to have sex with that they'd better make sure I had an orgasm. It was the late eighties so I imagine Rox was wearing something fluorescent, and it's likely that her earrings matched her socks. I was probably wearing a Def Leopard concert T-shirt. Or maybe it was this T-shirt I had back then that said "Sticks and stones may break my bones but whips and chains excite me." Oh, I really thought that was *sooo* witty when I was seventeen. Little did I know it was true! So, back to the list. We made one. And there were more pros than cons to doing it without waiting for love. And I finally had sex.

Making a list can help you organize your thoughts and figure out what you need. Some traits are probably more important than others. For instance, we might be attracted to certain physical traits or to a certain type of aesthetic, but that doesn't always mean we will get along and click with someone who meets those criteria. I can't tell you how many times some big butch girl has sent my snatch into hysterics, but as soon as we started talking my little mental hard-on died.

However, when we are attracted to someone's personality and the way they make us feel, then we find ourselves naturally drawn to them romantically and sexually. I hate to break it to you babes and butches out there who only want to date models, but thinking chicks must look like models makes you a modelizer. It means you have unrealistic expectations and need to grow up a little. I hate to be Captain Buzzkill, but I'm calling it like I see it.

OK, so let's look at some of your turn-ons. It's OK if a few of them are dorky or superficial. I mean, I love butches who ride motorcycles. And you can't get much more cliché than that. When the Dykes on Bikes contingent takes off in front of the dyke march every year I get so hot I have to practically run home and masturbate. If I were to make a list of my turn-ons, it would include things like nice hands, glasses, a sense of humor, cockiness.

10 things that turn me on

1.
2.
3.
4.
5.
6.
7.
8.
9.
10.

what are you attracted to?

This is especially important if you are new to dating women. Lesbian gender is kaleidoscopic. And if you've had little access to the wonderful world of queerdom, then it might just seem pretty mind-boggling. As you meet people and go on dates, you'll start to get an idea about what you are looking for. But figuring a few things out beforehand can help you feel more confident. Lots of women start their foray into dating other women by dating people who have a similar gender presentation to themselves only to discover as they became more confident and aware that they are actually attracted to people who are more masculine or feminine than they are.

what you want vs. what you need

Sometimes what you want doesn't line up with what you need. A want is a strong desire. A need is something you require for your physical and psychological well-being. You may have a fantasy person in mind who possesses all the traits you've listed as turn-ons, but some of those traits may be unrealistic for a serious relationship. For instance, if you're attracted to very gregarious, outgoing, social people, but you don't really like to go out every night, you may run into conflict. If you feel insecure or fear being abandoned if your partner likes to go out on her own, then you may need someone who is capable of making you feel secure and enjoys staying in as many nights as you do.

If you have been in previous relationships, ask yourself what your previous partner did and didn't do that made you happy. Did you have needs that went unmet? For instance, did you find yourself needing more positive feedback from your partner than you got? Or were you mismatched in some fundamental way like spiritually or financially? Are you happier when you are with someone who takes the lead or do you prefer making the decisions? Do you work a lot and need to be with someone who understands that about you? Are you ready to settle down and can't handle dating someone who wants to sleep around? Think about your needs as well as your wants when conjuring up your ideal date.

what are your deal breakers?

Knowing what doesn't work for you can also help define what you are looking for. It can really be hard to figure out without going through it. I've had many affairs and now I can look back on a lot of them and see how they would never have worked in the long term. That's not to say that I wasn't having fun and learning about myself and sex and all that good stuff while it was happening. But thinking about these things before you delve into the world of dates can help you figure out where to start.

If I were to make my own list of turn-offs it would include folk music, constantly getting really trashed, flakiness, internalized homophobia, and sexual repression. These things are deal breakers for me. I don't care how brilliant, gorgeous, well hung or exciting someone is. If she is always trashed, flakes out when we make plans, or gets freaked out and uncomfortable around sex, is transphobic or classist, then no matter how hot I find them physically, I know we won't get along.

10 things that turn me off

1.
2.
3.
4.
5.
6.
7.
8.
9.
10.

unlearn everything your mother taught you

IF YOU WERE raised as a girl, then you probably got a lot of confusing information about dating and gender roles. You were probably taught to be demure, play hard to get, wait for the other person to make the first move, and all sorts of other traits that do little to enhance your dating life.

Well, you are an adult now. Or at least you are close enough to being an adult that you are going to start dating. So throw all that stuff out. Just trash it and start over. Create your own set of rules about dating and sex. Go with what works for you and what makes you feel good about yourself.

It's important to have good boundaries and to set up guidelines for keeping yourself safe and happy both physically and emotionally. I'm not saying that your dating life needs to be a free-for-all. But I am definitely suggesting that you let go of outdated ways of thinking that do nothing but hold you back. One of the many beautiful things about being queer is getting to look at things from a fresh perspective because the established dating and relationship paradigms don't apply to same-gender or same-sex dating.

outdated ideas about dating

"I should only go out with people if I'm ready to settle down."

"Sleeping with more than one person is not allowed."

"I should only have sex if I'm in love."

"All relationships must last forever."

"I should wait for someone to ask me out."

"I'm not worthwhile without a partner."

"It's not OK to be aggressive."

"It's not OK to ask for what I want in bed."

"I should save myself for someone serious."

"I must be swept off my feet."

dating before you're ready

DON'T UNLEASH YOURSELF on the dyke dating world if you're going to do nothing but leave a trail of broken hearts. Everyone likes a challenge, but being hung up on an ex or otherwise occupied is a sure way to find yourself navigating a series of unpleasant and difficult dating situations. If you are unavailable, people fall for you. And having people who you aren't that into falling for you is not at all fun. So if you aren't over your ex, then go home and watch an Anne Heche movie or something on LOGO until you feel available.

wash that ex right out of your hair

Are you single? Are you really single? *Really?* Are you sure? Because if you are still processing your last relationship, then I have news for you, honey: You are *not* single. And if you trick anyone into thinking you are, then you'd better negotiate nonmonogamy, because you are still seeing your ex.

Are you bringing your ex along every time you go on a date? Being wrapped up in relationships that have long since ended is one of the biggest ways to sabotage any kind of dating life. Talking about your ex while on a date with someone else is just plain bad form. And processing about prior relationships can scare off even the most ardent suitor. No one wants to hear how you and your ex fought constantly. And extreme negative feelings about an ex girlfriend can indicate to a potential lover that you aren't really over that person. If you care enough about them to hate them, they are still playing a significant role in your life. And that will be communicated to your new special friend, and I'd be surprised if they wanted to take your ass out again.

Everyone's a little crazy sometimes, and dykes, bless their horny little hearts, are no exception to this rule. I remember a story my pal Bridget told me about being on a date with some girl she picked up online. They were having a perfectly nice evening when the conversation turned to discussing previous relationships and Bridget asked her dinner companion how long ago her last relationship had ended, the girl replied, "Tuesday."

I think we've all had that urge to run right out and fill up that empty space that our ex-girlfriend or ex-boyfriend has just left. It's like having a paper-doll cutout sitting there in our lives. And we're looking around for something vaguely girlfriend-shaped with which to plug up the whole. But moving from one relationship to the next means we don't really have the time to close down the feelings we had for the person we were just with. It takes time to move on.

beware the newly single!

The very newly single are unlike you and me. They are brain-, heart-, snatch-eating zombies. They have bad boundaries, intimacy issues, needs you will never be able to meet, unresolved anger, fucked-up living situations, weird fashion. I could go on. Any newly single person is capable of redeeming themselves and becoming a viable dating option. But she needs time to work that out. It doesn't happen overnight.

We have a tendency in our community to partner up pretty quickly. And as soon as we get out of something, we start looking for people to move up in the queue of crushes we invariably have and take the place of the last person. How many times have you broken up with someone and started interviewing potentials right away? You've done it. Admit it. We all have.

Here's the problem with dating the newly single: They aren't ready. But they will try to convince you that they are. And they will be convincing. In fact they will be so convincing you'll think

you have finally met someone without intimacy issues.
you've met someone who isn't afraid of becoming attach

They seem ready to fall in love, even to cohabitate and start adopting children. Let me tell you why this is. They are experiencing an intimacy hangover. Essentially they are still wrapped up in the level of closeness they experienced with their ex. And they haven't yet figured out that intimacy has to be rebuilt over time with a new person. Instead they think they can just fit you into that empty space.

Essentially the newly single aren't really single. They are still busy breaking up with their last girlfriend. Half the time they are still living together. Especially in metropolitan areas where apartments are harder to find and more expensive, a couple will break up but continue living in the same space, claiming they are just friends. And possibly even trying to date new people while still sharing a bed.

Or maybe it's not that bad—maybe she's gone, moved out, moved to the other side of the country, whatever. But psychically, for your potential date, that ex is still right there on her side of the bed criticizing the poor girl on her sexual technique, or telling her she needs a haircut, or purposefully shrinking her silk panties in the dryer. It's not pretty.

It takes time to resolve a relationship. Even a healthy relationship and an amicable breakup take time to fade.

too many women, too little time: don't rush things

Another bump in the road to happy dating is the urge to jump right in and get to know a million people at once. Once you've gotten your self-esteem intact, figured out what you are looking for, freed yourself from your previous relationships, and put yourself on the market, single ladies are likely to start approaching you or at the very least making it obvious that they are available. Having a glut of options is bound to make your head spin. Even if you live in a small town with no established lesbian community, once you start looking around, lots of single interested chicks are out there. They might not live next door, but get online and you will find that there are plenty of them to choose from. And that's where the trouble starts. You may start feeling like there are too many choices and you don't know how to date them all.

First of all, don't get carried away. Lesbians aren't going to suddenly disappear. And being a little bit unavailable just makes you seem more attractive. Getting carried away is really more of a problem when you are dating online than if you are meeting people through friends or social groups. With online dating people can start booking two and three dates in a night. While this might be a good way to meet as many people as possible, it also makes dating seem like a part-time job. You are supposed to be enjoying this game, not trying to meet a quota. It may feel a little overwhelming to have more than one suitor or crush. And while it's perfectly fine to date more than one person at a time, getting too wrapped up in meeting multiple people can keep you from focusing on the one person who may be right for you.

Keep in mind, dating chicks gets complicated fast. I don't care if you are butch, femme, neither, both, whatever. Girls talk. They talk amongst themselves about who they are dating, they compare notes, they gossip. This is especially true if you are living in an active lesbian community. Dating around is fun, but it's also a good way to get your name written on the bathroom wall of the local watering hole. So don't go tramping around breaking hearts because eventually you'll run low on options and everyone in town will have heard all about you.

CHAPTER 3

gender

SEX IS WHAT'S going on between your legs. But gender is what's going on in your head. And those two things don't always match up. What makes a person male or female? Is it external or internal? And what about masculine or feminine? Not all males are masculine nor are all females feminine. For the most part the concepts of masculine and feminine are still pretty up for discussion and seem to change every day. What we think of as masculine and feminine traits are largely constructed, meaning we pretty much made them up. There's no right or wrong way to be masculine or feminine. Many of us feel closer to one end of the spectrum than the other in terms of masculinity or femininity, but we may not see ourselves as a masculine or feminine person. Also keep in mind that masculine and feminine don't always line up with male and female. And anyone can have both masculine and feminine traits, regardless of gender.

The point is that our gender is not an absolute. It's mutable and complex.

For some of us a discussion of gender is irrelevant. We have female bodies. We fall in love with other female bodies and that's the end of it. We don't worry about gender roles. We hang our own shelves, pay for our own meals, and wear whatever we want without giving it a second thought. The hetero world may assign us gender based on the way we move through life and claim we are taking on a male role when we act aggressively, excel at sports, run large companies, or wear short hair. But we know we're beyond that type of thinking.

For some of us our gender is the core of our queerness. Gender is an important component to desire, how we see ourselves, and how we want to be seen. Our gender traits have little to do with what's in our panties. We may experience ourselves as female, but we know that our female experience looks nothing like that of straight women. Some women don't think of their bodies as specifically male or female. They think of themselves as androgynous and find a conversation about gender to be reductive and unnecessary. But to another person gender is highly relevant because her gender is at odds with the way the rest of the world perceives her. You can have a female body but experience your entire vulva as a cock and balls, or perhaps you think of your clit as a cock and your vagina as nonexistent. Your tits could be a chest or possibly not there at all. Or you could be totally at home in your female body but feel masculine and want your lovers to see you as such. You aren't male—you are a masculine female and that distinction is very important to you and the women you love.

You could also have been born with male body parts but experience your body as female. Your cock is a clit, you have breasts, hips, a G spot, maybe you think of your ass as a cunt. You want your lovers to see your body the way you experience it.

We may have been raised to present ourselves one way to the world but feel as if we should be presenting another way. Perhaps our parents dressed us up in bows and dresses and as soon as we are old enough to assert ourselves we throw out our girly clothes and start shopping in the boys' department.

Sometimes our gender distinctions are subtler. Some women feel very female but would never be comfortable in high femme attire. We wear pants and low-heeled shoes, go for low-maintenance hairstyles and think makeup looks like drag. And then there are high femmes who would feel stripped of their sexuality if you took away their stilettos. A high femme might have a carefully constructed feminine appearance, but you can be damn sure it doesn't make her weak or helpless.

In lesbian land gender is a pretty big deal. It's part of how we fuck and who we fuck. . We may all have similar parts downstairs, but the way we live with those parts ranges widely from person to person.

post-anatomy

The whole concept of your sexual orientation as defined by your anatomy has completely gone out the window. Back in the day it was simple. If there was a dick and a pussy involved, you were straight. If you had a dick and the person you were doing it with had a dick, you were a gay man. And if there were two pussies in your bed, you were a lesbian. Now you can be a transgendered male with a cunt and tits doing it with a bio gay boy who has a cock. Maybe your anatomy says you are having hetero sex, but in reality nothing could be further from the truth.

We can't even define what it means to be a lesbian anymore. In this day and age we are post-lesbian. Are transmen lesbians? What about transwomen? Are high femmes who date butches lesbians? What about two butch dykes who think of their strap-ons as cocks? They might both also have pussies but they may not think of themselves as being in a lesbian relationship.

In the early nineties Cindy Crawford in a suit was scandalous. Then in the mid nineties it was all about androgynyand bluring gender or just ignoring it. Madonna was flirting with Sandra Bernhard, Sandra Bernhard was flirting with gay men, Sinead O'Connor came out of the closet and then went back in and then everyone forgot she even existed. A few years later Madonna was wearing suits and pretending to be the butch to Christina Aguilera's and Britney Spears' femme. And now here we are in the twenty-first century and gender is more hard to define than it has ever been. Our gender identity can shift and change over the course of a lifetime. We may feel one way about ourselves for years and then gradually or even suddenly grow into a differently gendered creature. Our gender identity affects our queer identity and so many of the terms we've used over the years no longer really apply. The words gay, bi, and lesbian have collected so many meanings over the years that many people who used to identify this way find themselves feeling boxed in by what other people's notions of these terms are. More and more umbrella terms like "queer" get thrown around in lieu of gay and lesbian. And some people just choose not to identify at all. .

what does this have to do with dating?

In lesbian land gender is often tied in with the way we want to fuck or get fucked, who we want to date, how we want to dress, or who we want to hang out with. Most of us understand that gender exists on a continuum, but it's also important to recognize that masculine and feminine also exist on a continuum. There are many, many ways to be masculine—and just as many ways to be feminine. Remember that discussion we had in chapter one about how no one has to be the "boy"? Well, when we worry about who is the boy, what we really mean is who does the paying? Who carries the heavy things, who does the driving, who is the aggressor in bed, who wears the pants, who earns more money? Or who does the cooking and cleaning? Who raises the kids, decorates the apartment, and who is the receptive partner in bed? Just because you are feminine doesn't mean you are necessarily passive, maternal, or weak.

We've assigned some traits to masculinity and some to femininity. And when a woman or a man adopts a role outside of what we consider normal, we think of it as transgressive. A lot of homophobia stems from gender transgression. Homophobes don't like the idea that women are taking on what they see as male roles by being strong, sexually aggressive, and—god forbid!—having a dick.

We may opt to express our gender identity through the way we dress. A very feminine woman may wear a skirt and heels to work because she feels as if she's not really dressed when she's wearing pants. But some of us don't express our gender through our outward appearance because we worry that people won't accept us as we see ourselves. A transwoman may dress in male drag for work because she isn't able to be out in her workplace, but that doesn't make her any less female. And a butch dyke might wear a dress to her sister's wedding, but she's still butch.

One of the beauties of being queer is being able to construct your presentation of gender in any way you want. High femmes often complain that because they are very feminine no one sees how much work has gone into the creation of their gender and sexual identity. We see "femme" as a default identity to people born with tits. But femininity is no more a default than anything else. Babies may be born with female anatomy, but they sure as hell aren't born with six-inch platform heels and false eyelashes.

throw out your expectations: intersexuality

JUST BECAUSE YOU have tits and a cunt doesn't mean you have to experience those parts the same way your girlfriend does. Your anatomy doesn't dictate your gender. In fact, in the case of intersexed individuals, your anatomy sometimes doesn't even accurately indicate your sex.

According to the Intersex Society of North America (ISNA) one baby out of every 500 is born with characteristics of both sexes. These babies have some other combination of chromosomes besides XX or XY and often suffer the misfortune of having their sex "assigned" for them by medical professionals. How do doctors decide which sex a baby is? Well, it all comes down to dick size—doesn't everything? If a clit is bigger than three-eighths of an inch, it's considered alarmingly large and given the ol' snip-snip so that it will look more like what the parents and doctors consider normal. This often results in the surgically altered genitalia having reduced sensitivity. Even worse, this also often results in a child being assigned a sex that he or she doesn't really feel himself or herself to be. The idea behind surgery is that children must have a fixed gender identity and anatomy to match. But who's to say what a child's gender is? And are larger than average or smaller than average genitals really something that need fixing? What is the sexual and gender identity of an intersexed person? Are intersexed people queer? It varies from individual to individual.

genderqueer

Genderqueer is a term that has become a common part of the dyke vernacular. It's shorthand for gender that doesn't fit into the established paradigms. It means that a person doesn't see themselves as male or female or both or neither, but perhaps a combination of several genders or even as more than one sex. All sorts of queers identify as genderqueer, one of the reasons the term has become popular is that it is new enough that its not carrying a lot of baggage. Femmes with facial hair often identify as genderqueer. Sometimes dykes who have a lot of masculine traits that they feel are at odds with their female bodies identify as genderqueer. Genderqueers can also be boys or girls who feel that their way of experiencing masculinity and femininity is different from what they see on TV or were taught by their families. Really, "genderqueer" can apply to anyone who feels as if their gender identity is more complex than pink or blue. The whole idea of queerness and queer gender is that queers experience sex, desire, gender, and love in ways that don't fit established paradigms. And the fact that we have sex the way we do, and experience desire the way we do, implies that our gender doesn't meet standard hetero expectations. The term is widely used in our community, and many queer, dyke, gay, bi, and whatever-else-you-can-think-of individuals identify as genderqueer. It's a common umbrella term without a set meaning, and many people find that it feels more comfortable than some of the older and more established terms we use to decribe how we exist in the world.

gender-fluid

"Gender-fluid" is a way of describing our experience of gender as mutable and able to shift around to fit our moods, our environments, or even our outfits. Being gender-fluid is slightly different from being genderqueer. Being genderqueer means that your gender flies in the face of traditional gender experiences. But having a fluid gender means that the way you think of and present yourself can change from moment to moment.

transgenderism

The term "transgendered" covers any individual whose physical anatomy does not match his or her gender identity. The term is used for FTMs (female-to-male transfolk) and MTFs (male-to-female transfolk), but it can also apply to drag kings, faux queens, faux kings, drag queens, butch dykes, transvestites, cross-dressers, genderqueers, high femmes, and really anyone who considers their experience of gender to be different from accepted norms.

transmen

FTMs may opt to take testosterone in order to gain more masculine secondary sex characteristics such as facial hair, body hair, redistribution of body fat, and a deeper voice.

Some FTMs have top surgery, which involves a mastectomy and reshaping and replacing of the nipples in order to give their chests a more masculine appearance. Less common forms of surgical alteration for FTMs involve genital reconstructive surgery. Taking testosterone (usually called T) will cause the clitoris to grow to up to three inches in length. Surgical options for genital reconstruction include vaginectomy, which is the removal of the vagina, and metaoidioplasty, which frees the hormone-enhanced clit from the surrounding tissue and reshapes the tissue of the labia into a scrotal sac. Sometimes in metaoidioplasty the urethra is rerouted through the head of the clitoris so that transguys can pee out of their dicks. Phalloplasty, which is the creation of a phallus using skin grafts from other parts of the body, is the least common form of genital reconstruction because the results are often less than satisfactory. The procedure will sometimes involve implanting an inflatable prosthesis so that the newly constructed penis can get hard.

Lots of FTMs don't opt for any hormones or surgeries. These guys may bind their chests to give them a more masculine appearance, or not even that. Physiologically they may have female parts, but that doesn't make them female.

Transmen have various sexual identities: Some identify as straight men, some as bisexual, some still consider themselves dykes, and often transmen identify as simply queer.

transwomen

MTFs often take anti-androgens and estrogen resulting in a redistribution of body fat into a more typical female pattern, and a lessening of secondary male sexual characteristics like body and facial hair. Hormones also give MTFs a higher-pitched voice, breasts, softer skin, girlier hips, and a booty.

Some MTFs will opt for breast implants, though many women find that the breasts they grow from taking estrogen are enough.

Genital surgeries available to MTFs involve vaginoplasty and labiaplasty, in which the penis and scrotum are inverted and reshaped as a working vagina and sensitive clitoris. The new vag doesn't self-lubricate, but it does have sensation and is made of erectile tissue that engorges with arousal. It is usually capable of orgasm. MTFs who don't opt for surgery may find that taking estrogen keeps them from being able to get an erection. But that doesn't mean that they aren't experiencing arousal or are not sexually responsive. Often MTFs grew up at odds with their penises and never thought of them as the source of sexual arousal anyway. MTFs learn to rewire their sexual response so that they can experience orgasm in new and different ways.

Transwomen can date bio women or other transwomen and identify as lesbian, they can date both men and women and identify as bisexual, or they can identify as queer or straight or anything else they like.

butch-femme

"Butch-femme" can mean all sorts of things. For some of us it's an immutable set of rules that color every part of our queer life. For others it's simply a sexual dynamic, something that makes sex hotter. Butches and femmes find that yin-yang dynamic that exists between them to be an incredible draw.

What butch-femme sexuality means varies from butch to butch and femme to femme. Sometimes it means adopting typical male-female gender roles, which for most butch-femme couples feels very transgressive and kinky. Other times it simply means that one partner is more feminine and one partner is more masculine and they are drawn to the traits in each other that they don't see themselves as having.

Butches and femmes often play with very traditional roles, which in a queer context become really hot. The power dynamic is skewed in a butch-femme couple because no matter who adopts a masculine role and who adopts a feminine role, ultimately you have the same amount of power in greater society.

There is no right or wrong way to be butch or femme. Being butch doesn't mean you have to dress a certain way, act a certain way, or feel a certain way. Butches are still butch regardless of whether they are bottoms or tops, whether they play sports or enjoy cooking. And femmes are femme even if they prefer being dominant in bed, can change their own tires, and have no interest in having kids.

the bedroom

One of the mistakes we make most often is assuming things about someone's sexual roles based on their gender presentation. We see a high femme in full drag and assume she adopts a receptive role in bed, or that her butch partner is always on top. Gender presentation does not accurately reflect a person's sexual proclivities.

Butch-femme is more about a dynamic that exists between two people than it is a set of rules or guidelines. Butches and femmes are opposites that attract.

From women who passed as men in Victorian times to blue-collar butches in the fifties, butch-femme desire has been around as long as dykes have been around. A common critique of butch-femme identity is that it is aping heterosexual dynamics. However, dykes who identify as butch-femme know that their sexuality has nothing to do with aping anything at all. It's simply a way of experiencing desire that feels natural and essential. Butches might take on a masculine role, but that in no way implies they want to be men. Butch-femme empowers both butches and femmes by allowing them to inhabit a way of being female that flies in the face of heteronormativity.

Butch-femme is a very visible form of lesbian desire. Many women find that this type of sexual visibility is a statement in and of itself. Rather than mimicking hetero couples it's a loud and clear way of claiming power over our sexuality and how it is perceived. Traditionally in a butch-femme sexual dynamic the butches roles is to give pleasure to the femme, and the femmes role is to demand and receive sexual pleasure. This flies in the face of traditional gender roles where the man is the recipient of sexual gratification.

Butch-femme is changing and many of the traditional roles that came out of butch-femme in the forties and fifties are becoming less and less useful. Many butches and femmes still adopt rigid gender roles, but many do not.

If you are interested in butch-femme culture there are many places to find more information. I'd recommend starting with Joan Nestle's *The Persistent Desire: A Femme-Butch Reader*. There is so much wonderful literature about Butch-femme. Do a google search and head to the library. Maybe you'll get lucky in the queer reading room.

part two

the master dater

CHAPTER 4

where the girls are

BY THIS TIME you are probably thinking, OK, OK, I have good self-esteem, I like my body, I got a haircut, now show me to the pussy!

You know where dykes meet each other? Through other dykes. For one thing, we recycle exes. For another thing, we all know each other so we're good at fixing up friends with friends. If you are single and looking, make it known. Tell everyone you want to meet someone. Go to parties. Or throw a party. Tell all your friends that they have to bring along one person you don't know.

Joining an activity group of some kind expands your social circle dramatically. Start dropping in on your friend's book-club meetings, or get involved with the film festival. You'll meet new people whom you may be attracted to, and you'll also have access to all the people your new friends know, and you may find that you like one of them.

Are you a brand-spanking-new lesbian who doesn't know a lot of other dykes? It can be intimidating to break into a new scene. Especially a big group of lesbians because it probably seems like they all know each other. But that's just an act. It's posturing. It's not as hard to meet new gay ladies as you might think. Sure everyone is standing around trying to look cool. But really they are just as insecure and afraid of rejection as anyone else. Trust me on this.

Do you have an LGBT center in your town? If so, lucky you.

The center is a great place to meet freshly out gays new to the scene. Try going to a dance or taking a class. There will probably be a lot of other fresh new lesbians there looking to meet chicks like you. Are you in college? I met my first girlfriend in a lesbian literature class. Get out, get involved. Turn your flirt on and smile at every pretty girl you see. Worried they aren't gay? Who cares! Seduce them! Turning straight girls is the new black.

places to meet dykes

queer film festivals

erotica readings

sex parties

sex-toy stores

art openings

yoga

the gym

a women's studies class

dance clubs

bars

the library

a friend's house

pride festivals

activist groups

feminist organizations

lgbt organizations

twelve-step meetings

any queer-sponsored event

been there, done that

OK, SO MAYBE you've been around a while and everyone at the center just looks like chicken to you. I hear you, sister, been there myself. Have you already hit every queer booty in your town? And now you're single and bored and sick of waiting around for fresh meat to get off the bus? Turned all the straight ladies already? Then maybe what you need is a vacation. Head to the nearest women's weekend. There are women's events all over the country. Go buy yourself a *Damron Women's Traveller*. It will list every gay bar in every gay city across the gay USA. Not only that but it will list all the women's events all over the entire planet.

tried and true:
large-scale lesbian events

Like many overworked, underpaid young dykes, Sandy and Dawn wanted to take a cheap vacation where they could have fun, be as out as they are at home, and get their flirt on.

"We didn't want to go on vacation and feel isolated from other queers," says Sandy. "We knew we'd have fun wherever we went, but we wanted to make sure that it was a queer-friendly environment."

They checked out the *Damron Women's Traveller* for inspiration. A quick search of the "Events" section of the popular travel guide will give you a staggering number of places to go to hang out with other queers. From Pride celebrations to leather events, a dyke in the mood to party can go somewhere gay just about every week of the year. Sandy and Dawn decided to head for Womenfest, an annual women's party in Key West, Florida. It promised everything they hoped for: tropical locale, party atmosphere, and hotels full of lesbians.

Within hours of landing on the island of Key West the two twenty-somethings were getting shamelessly cruised by a group of horny, drunken ladies. "We walked onto the patio at Pearl's Rainbow, one of the women's B&Bs, and totally felt like prey," says Sandy. "I think people could tell we were out-of-towners. It was packed and we kind of had that fresh-meat syndrome going on a little."

Sandy pauses to sip her decaf latte. "Two days after we arrived, I was sitting in a restaurant having brunch with a girl I met the night before when I realized that the girl I had a date with for that very night was about to take our order." She continues, "I honestly couldn't believe how sexy Key West was. I never get action like that at home. I think the fact that I was on vacation and would probably never see either of these girls again allowed me to act really aggressively."

Agreeing that vacation rules up the odds, Regina, a 31-year-old facilities manager at a large advertising agency, says, "I've gotten laid pretty much every time I've gone to Palm Springs," referring to the Dinah Shore weekend, one of the largest lesbian events in the country. "Lesbian events are like a forced party. It's a very see-and-be-seen kind of atmosphere. And it's not really authentic. But the fact that everyone feels like they are on display means that they act a little crazier than they would normally."

So can single lesbians expect to show up at a women's party and start collecting phone numbers? Regina believes that the fact that everyone is drinking and bikini-clad is what makes Dinah Shore such a sex-charged event. The atmosphere lends itself to sexually aggressive behavior. "I don't like to hit on women," she explains. "I usually just wait until someone approaches me, and inevitably they do. I met a girl while sitting by the pool. We made eye contact across a crowd and she came over and sat on the edge of my chair. We started making out right there in front of everyone until people started applauding! Later that night we had sex in the back of my car. It was great until the next day when she spotted me with someone else and made a huge scene. I was really glad when it was time to go home."

Leather events are another option for hooking up on the road. Ian, a 40-something leather dyke, says that not all events are created equal, but generally if she sees someone who sparks her interest, she's usually successful in getting them to play. The big problem is when people are too shy to approach each other. "The most successful event I've attended was WALP, the women's leather pride celebration in Amsterdam. Essentially the reason it worked so well was because a really tall German leather dyke took control and assigned people to each other. She stood in the center of the room and pointed to different women and said, 'You play with her, you play with her.' And everyone had a great time."

"I think the Michigan Womyn's Music Festival is a great place to meet women," says Grace, a 39-year-old dyke, of the well-known yearly music-and-camping event with about 5,000 attendees. "I've attended every year for the past four years and to me it seems like the place is crawling with sexual energy. I think if you are interested in fooling around opportunities will present themselves."

Not all dykes love women's events, however. Susanna, a 30-year-old mechanical engineer with gorgeous eyes and a high-femme aesthetic, says, "I never do well at women's events. I think these events are poorly attended by people with extreme genders like I am. The only time I've ever met anyone is when I've left the event out of frustration and gone somewhere else." Irena attended her first Michigan Women's Music Festival in August 2005. "It was disappointing. I'd heard so many stories about Mich-fest hookups and how there were play parties every night. But in reality I felt isolated. It's almost like there was too much choice. I felt overwhelmed and withdrawn."

"Admittedly part of the problem was that I was turned off by everyone's camping attire," explains Susanna. "I was traveling with my housemate Rose and at the end of the week we were tired of camping. We caught a ride off 'the land' and stayed overnight in a hotel in Grand Rapids. Rose actually picked a girl up in the hotel bar and took her back to the room. We both had more luck in a random hotel bar than in a designated women's space attended by thousands of lesbians!"

So are women's weekends the answer to your hook-up prayers? "It depends on what you're looking for and where you go," says Amy, a New York party promoter. "I've certainly had some great times at lesbian events, but sometimes the drinking and craziness can get a little over-the-top. I've thrown parties where women have gotten so crazy that fights have broken out, and I've also attended events that were poorly attended and kind of boring. I'd say if you are ready to get really wild and let down your inhibitions, there are many events, especially summer ones, where you can make that happen. Your best bet is to ask around and get information from other dykes before you go."

hit the web to find out more info about women's events in your area

www.michfest.org
www.womenfest.com
www.dinahshoreweekend.com

the bar scene

ASK THE DYKES you know and a good portion of them will probably tell you their first experiences with other queer women took place in lesbian bars. A dyke bar is the one place you can go and safely assume everyone inside is a homo. Dyke bars are where a lot of us came out, and where a lot of us still go on a pretty regular basis. The newly gay may not know about everything going on in the queer lady scene, but you bet they know where the dyke bars are. Bars are a great place to go when you just want to be around other homos.

Dyke bars can be sexy and fun, and if you live in a city with a big gay community, there are probably lots of events going on in various gay bars around town. There are probably more parties and clubs being held at bars than any other type of establishment. As my mom likes to say, the gays know how to party. Plus, let's face it, drinking is fun and makes it a whole lot easier to get laid. And let's not forget that drinking makes people more attractive—at least until you sober up.

Up until Phyllis Lyon and Del Martin formed the Daughters of Bilitis in the fifties, bars were where chicks met each other. That's really all there was. And queer culture was bar culture. Phyllis and Del wanted lesbians to have other options; they saw alcoholism wrecking the community, and they formed a social group so that dykes would have a something else to do besides drink themselves silly.

But even though we now have many, many options for meeting fine ladies, the bar still reigns supreme. Dykes hang out at the dyke bar. No, not all of them. And in fact the dykes who are spending tons of time in the bar probably don't have a lot going on in their lives and you might want to think twice about getting serious with them. But plenty of perfectly nice chicks are hanging out at the gay bar, and if you want to meet some, it's a good bet.

Want to find out where the ladies' nights are in your neighborhood? Pick up your local gay rag and check out the listings. Or hit the Internet. Parties get posted as Myspace bulletins and on Craigslist. Lots of cities have local listings online; do a Google search and find an online resource. Or check the *Damron Women's Traveller* to find all the gay-bar listings in your locale.

the club scene

Clubbing sounds like something terrible that happens to baby seals, but really it means just going out dancing and probably drinking a lot of vodka and Red Bull. Clubs are where the big weekly and monthly parties are held, and are usually a "sceney dress-up and cruise" atmosphere rather than a "sit at the bar in your flannel shirt and knock back a PBR or ten" kind of a night.

Clubs are a good place to meet chicks. I'm not sure they are a great place to meet the love of your life. But what is? The point is that the club scene is often a very sexually charged atmosphere; people are hot and sweaty from dancing and ingesting various substances, and inhibitions get thrown right out the window.

There's a kind of mass insanity to a club atmosphere when all the elements are in place. Dance floors become transcendental, and people get moved along by music and proximity to so many other bodies and sex and who knows what else. And the next thing you know you are falling in love with every person you see while Madonna is speaking directly to you through the DJ, telling you that you are glamorous and young and beautiful and so is everyone else and you should all just have sex right then and there. Regardless, a good party with a good DJ can be a great place to get your dance on. New York throws the best parties, but if you don't live there find a local gay rag and check out the listings. If there are no good parties, round up all the dykes you know and hit the boy bars. Gay boys throw the best parties.

playing with boys

Another place to meet dykes is in the gay-boy scene. There's always a handful of dykes hanging out in the boy bars playing pool with their buddies, or just getting away from their dyke drama for the night. Hanging out with boys is nice because you still get to be in a very queer environment, but not necessarily as on display as you're in a crowded lesbian bar. Having gay-guy friends is very necessary to your survival in the dating world. Guy friends can fix you up with friends of theirs, help you get dressed for dates, play wing man when you are too shy to approach someone on your own, and provide a lesbian-free environment to hang out in when you have a bad breakup and need some space.

a queer cocktail primer

THE LEXINGTON AND El Rio are two of the most packed dyke bars in all of San Francisco. And Robin Akimbo and Jess Arndt are two of the hottest bartenders from those bars. The two lovely mixologists sat down with me over some morning-after Bloody Marys to share some bartender wisdom with those of us who need a little help handling the demon alcohol. Here is their advice for you about cocktail consumption.

What's a good drink to order if you want to appear smooth for your date?

ROBIN: For ladies I think a cocktail is impressive. Especially if you know what you want it mixed with and how you want it poured. But for butches a cocktail is a little fey.

JESS: Though butches can get away with ordering a

cocktail in a rocks glass or a tumbler. A lot of people don't want to hold a martini glass. Knowing what you want to drink and ordering it confidently is key.

What should you avoid ordering if you don't want to look stupid?

ROBIN: Tropical drinks. People have ordered Pina Coladas at the Lexington before. We aren't in Cancun and I can't crack open a fresh coconut. I'm just going to pull some nasty mixer off the back of the shelf.

DIANA: Yeah, nothing like a Pina Colada on a cold foggy day in a dark San Francisco dyke bar.

JESS: Order classic cocktails. Stay away from fruity tropical things—they make you look like a kid. If you want something sweet, order something old-fashioned like a French martini instead. Or order bourbon on the rocks.

What's a French martini?

JESS: It's vodka, Chambord, and pineapple. Also, sidecars are very cool. And again, if you don't want to hold a martini glass, you can ask for it in a tumbler. A sidecar is cognac, cointreau, and lemon juice in a glass with a sugared rim.

ROBIN: Also, I just want to add that you have to really like bourbon if you are going to order it. Don't order something you don't like because you think it makes you look cool.

What do people order if they want to get laid?

JESS: Shots.

ROBIN: Shots.

Do they order shots for themselves or for their date?
JESS: You can't just order shots for your date.

You mean you can't order yourself a beer and then say, "And she'll have six kamikazes and a roofie?"
JESS: People start ordering shots when they are ready to get the party started.
ROBIN: But it's important to stick with what you know so you don't get wasted. If you are going to order shots, tread carefully.

What should you do if your date gets really trashed?
JESS: You should probably end your date. Make sure they have a safe way to get home. Ask the bartender to call a cab. And basically just make sure that she's all right. Whatever you do, don't take her home and have sex with her when she's trashed.
ROBIN: And call her the next morning to check in. She probably feels embarrassed.

What's a good way to make sure you don't get drunk and make an ass of yourself?
JESS: Eat before you go out. And then order club soda in between cocktails. If you are going to be out all night, make sure you drink a lot of water.
ROBIN: Don't experiment with new cocktails.

How do you meet girls in bars? Is it cool to buy someone a drink?
ROBIN: You mean cold? Without knowing them at all? It's a pretty ballsy move. I don't suggest it.
JESS: You can enlist the bartender's help. It's OK to ask what she's drinking and if she's alone or with a date.

ROBIN: I would try talking to her before I offered her a drink. If you send a drink over to her she'll feel obligated.

Yeah, that's true. I never know what to do when people send me drinks. I usually just have sex with them right there at the bar. That brings me to my next question. Is it OK to have sex in the bathroom? Or is that just too trashy?

ROBIN: It's better than doing it in front of everyone.

JESS: People get crazy. I've witnessed fisting scenes at Mango [a popular San Francisco dyke dance party]. I feel like you should go to the bar and have fun and drink a little but maybe go to your house before you do anything as involved as fisting.

ROBIN: Making out a little at the bar is hot, but going much further than kissing is risky. I've asked people to leave the Lexington because they were fucking and it was making people uncomfortable.

JESS: Don't make out on the pool table. It's really tacky. It might feel really hot to you, but probably everyone else just wants to play pool.

Is there anything else we need to know?

JESS: Don't get drunk and hit on the bartender.

ROBIN: Yes, I'm busy after my shift.

are you sober?

You know where else dykes are? They are in recovery. If you are sober, head to a twelve-step meeting in your town. I think you'll find that there are plenty of other queer women in recovery and they can be a source of friendship, support, affection, and sometimes love and sex.

People are always asking me about what they perceive to be the high level of substance abuse, depression, trauma, violence, sexual abuse, and other painful issues that exist in the queer community. It's my belief that queers don't necessarily have a disproportionate amount of these problems, but because we are used to dealing with feeling like an "other" in society, we are more willing to talk openly about things that the rest of the world prefers to keep suppressed.

If you are sober, connect with other sober women and hang out in substance-free spaces together.

the leather scene

I love leather dykes, bless their kinky little hearts. And if you are at all curious about BDSM, or kinky sex play, or even just like the outfits, the leather community in your town can be a great place to score sex partners. The leather community is throwing all the good sex parties; they are holding the meetings, teaching the workshops, planning the scenes, negotiating boundaries. I mean, those babes are prepared. There are leather and sex events, and women's BDSM groups all over the country. Get online and do a little research—you might learn a few things about yourself.

check these websites for more information about leather events:

www.lesbiansexmafia.com
www.the-exiles.org
www.theleatherpage.com

sporting events, a hotbed of lezzie activity

IF YOU ARE athletically inclined, you probably don't need me to tell you that sporting events are like lesbian sex parties only people aren't wearing the uniforms ironically. Remember high school when you weren't out yet, but you were strangely attracted to everyone on the field hockey team? Yeah, me, too.

If you play sports, join a women's sports team or a league—or just start showing up at games. It doesn't really matter what sport. The thing that the WNBA is trying to keep on the down low is that the majority of female athletes are dykes, or at least willing to learn.

If you don't play sports, hang out where the chick athletes hang out. Find the bar they all go to after their game. Or hang out in the park where they practice. In San Francisco the women's flag football league has its own cheerleaders. You can totally fulfill your high school fantasy of becoming head cheerleader and banging the captain of the football team, only the sex will be far better.

Want to seduce a sporty dyke but don't know the first thing about sports? Ask her to explain the rules of softball or football to you. Or ask her to teach you to throw or surf or whatever her specialty is. If you are lucky, the lesson will include a lot of her having to wrap her nice, muscular, athletic arms around you.

I'm not an athlete in any way—I wear heels so much my feet are Barbie shaped. But over the course of my dating life I've been involved with several football players, a softball player, a surfer, and a basketball player. Dykes love sports, I'm telling you.

the internet is your friend

AND NOW WE get to the mother of all places to meet chicks, the World Wide Interweb. Everyone is online. And everyone is cruising online personals at their desk while pretending to work.

Craigslist is everywhere. You can post a women-seeking-women ad on the Craigslist in Indonesia before your next vacation if you are so inclined. And Myspace is not only free, it's absolutely full of dyke drama. It's like a virtual lesbian bar. Thanks to Myspace, every lesbian you know is spying on every other lesbian you know from the comfort of their own bed.

writing a personal ad

Craigslist is a good place to start. Write yourself an ad stating what you are looking for. Be specific about your needs and wants. Remember that list you made in chapter two of the things that turned you off and the things that turned you on? Well now is the time to employ it.

personal ad examples

I pulled these ads off Craigslist. The first two ads are good examples of people knowing exactly what they want. The last ad is open to interpretation.

"Hot sick ftm boy seeks dominant creative experienced femme top or switch. I am easy on the eyes, experienced, sweet, extremely perverted, love to play hard. Good communicator, no drama. ageplay A+"

"SWF seeks same. I'll be damned if there isn't a significant amount of energy that I need released! It's been a long time since this babygirl has gotten down and dirty, and it's about time. I prefer femmes, I am a femme, let's keep it femme. I love to top, I love my strap-on, I love to be submissive, and I love your strap-on. I'm damn cute. Long hair, great skin, a little on the thicker side, curves in the right places and willing to share a G-rated photo upon receiving your e-mail, and your picture."

"So I'm not looking for much here. All I want is to maybe go on a few dates with some cute, friendly, honest, 420 friendly, cool girls. I don't expect to find 'the one' here, but I'd love to try. Hell, if nothing else there's dinner, maybe drinks and hopefully some great company! I'm very much into femme girls, but hey a date is a date. If there is no chemistry so be it, we can still have a freaking blast! If you have a pic send it along."

how to read a personal ad

Be warned. Not everyone tells the truth in personal ads. To keep from getting any nasty surprises, first consult my handy dandy personal ad decoder to make sure you get what you want.

IF IT SAYS: I need a girl to come over and get me off
IT MEANS: My boyfriend wants to watch us have sex

IF IT SAYS: I'm always on top
IT MEANS: I have control issues

IF IT SAYS: Big bad daddy
IT MEANS: I have unresolved masculinity issues

IF IT SAYS: Just looking for phone sex
IT MEANS: I have an STD

IF IT SAYS: Bi-curious girly girl looking for same
IT MEANS: My boyfriend cheated on me

acronym cheat sheet

Compiled from Craigslist, and several other Internet dating sites, here are most of the acronyms you'll need to decipher personal ads.

A: Asian, for second letter of a three-letter acronym (TLA)

B: Bisexual, for first letter of a TLA

B: Black, for second letter of a TLA

F: Female, for third letter of a TLA

G: Gay, for first letter of a TLA

J: Jewish or Japanese, for second letter of a TLA

L: Latino or Latina, for second letter of a TLA

M: Male, for third letter of a TLA

M: Man, used before or after 4

T: Transgender, used before or after 4

W: White, for second letter of a TLA

W: Woman, used before or after 4

4: For or Looking For

420 (OR 4:20): Cannabis

B&D (ALSO B/D): Bondage and Discipline

BB: Body-Builder or Barebacking

BBC: Big Black Cock

BBW: Big Beautiful Woman

BDSM: Bondage and Discipline, Domination and Submission, Sadomasochism

BF: Black Female, or Boy Friend

BI: Bisexual

BIF: Bisexual Female

BIM: Bisexual Male

CD: Cross Dresser

D/D: Drug and Disease

DOM: Male Dominant partner/participant in BDSM

DOMME: Female Dominant partner/participant in BDSM

D/S: Domination and Submission, lowercase s signifies power exchange

DTE: Down-to-earth

FTM: Female-to-Male Transgender

GBM: Gay Black Male

GF: Gay Female (Lesbian), or Girl Friend

GG: Genetic Girl/Real Girl/All-Girl as opposed to a TV/TS/TG "girl"

GHM: Gay Hispanic Male

GWC: Gay White Couple

GWF: Gay White Female

GWM: Gay White Male

HET: Heterosexual

HWP: Height Weight Proportional: indicates an "ideal" body weight

IRL: In Real Life: face-to-face meeting

ISO: In Search Of

LTR: Long-Term Relationship

M4M: Man Looking For Man

M4MW: Man Looking for Man and Woman

M4T: Male Looking for Transsexual or Transvestite (Cross Dresser)

M4W: Man Looking for Woman

MBC: Married Black Couple

MBIC: Married Bisexual Couple

MHC: Married Hispanic Couple

MOTOS: Member of the Opposite Sex

MOTSS: Member of the Same Sex

MTF: Male-to-Female Transgender

MW4M: Man and Woman Looking for Man

MW4MW: Man and Woman Looking for Man and Woman

MW4W: Man and Woman Looking for Woman

MWC: Married White Couple

NS: Non-Smoking

NSA: No Strings Attached

PNP: Party and Play (drugs, usually crystal meth, and sex)

PRE-OP: Pre-Operational Transsexual with genitalia unaltered, typically male-to-female

RTS: Real-Time Sex

S&M (ALSO S/M): Sadomasochism

SAE: Self-Addressed Envelope

SASE: Self-Addressed Stamped Envelope

SBF: Single Black Female

SBM: Single Black Male

SBIF: Single Bisexual Female

SBIM: Single Bisexual Male

SNOW: Cocaine

STD: Sexually Transmitted Disease

SWF: Single White Female

SWM: Single White Male

STR8: Straight (not bisexual or gay)

SUB (ALSO SUBBY OR SUBBIE): Submissive partner/participant TG: Transgendered person

TINA: Crystal Methamphetamine

TS: (also Transsexual or Tranny) Transsexual person, typically male-to-female

TV: Transvestite person

TLC: Tender Loving Care

W/E: Well Endowed: larger than average cock

W/S: Watersports

W4M: Woman Looking For Man

some online dating sites

Nerve.com

Butchfemmepersonals.com

Butchfemmematchmaker.com

Curve.com

Lavelife.com

Personals.yahoo.com

Match.com

Jdate.com

Gay.com

OkCupid.com

AmericanSingles.com

EHarmony.com

Webdate.com

Tickle.com

True.com

PerfectMatch.com

BlackPlanet.com

FriendFinder.com

lust online: social networking for the single and sexy

FORGET DILDOS. WHAT we really need are strap-on iBooks.

A tall girl wearing a white T-shirt and jeans leans against the wall at a popular San Francisco leather bar. The crowd is mixed; a lot of men in chaps and a scattered number of dykes are smoking on the back patio. "I met her on Craigslist," she says in reference to her latest trick. "She was visiting the Bay Area for a medical conference. She placed an ad saying that she was looking for fun while she was here and I thought she sounded pretty hot. We exchanged photos and she was a little straight-looking for my usual taste, but I guess that's because she works for a pharmaceutical company. We had fun in her hotel room." Her friend nods and swigs from a Corona, then says "Craigslist is a good place to hook up with out-of-towners. I already have a primary relationship, but my girlfriend and I play with other people. I prefer to meet others online where it's understood that it's a one-time thing."

For years now those of us looking for a little strange have turned to Craigslist. The Women-Seeking-Women section is heavily trolled in major metropolitan areas from San Diego to D.C., and a simple "Butch Seeking Femme" ad can garner fifty responses by the next morning. A recent search of the site turned up two postings seeking information about queer Starbucks Baristas working in the financial district, one posting from someone looking specifically for a regular lunch-time habit, an ongoing discussion about oral sex techniques, and an array of requests for everything from a butch boi bottom to a femme of size in need of boot service. "Craigslist is like ordering a pizza," says Laurel, a 26-year-old grad student. "Most of the people on dating sites like Gay.com are looking for a relationship, and that isn't really what I'm into right now. I've found hookups, a boyfriend, furniture, and an apartment on Craigslist." Laurel, a queer trannyboy bottom who uses Craigslist to find butch and FTM tops explains that Craigslist revolutionized his sex life. "What I want is so specific, it's just easier to find it online, meet up for coffee, decide if you like each other and then go back to an apartment and fuck."

Dykes with day jobs have found that the Internet allows us to cruise for sex while filing expense reports, but it has also changed the way we interact. "I love that I don't have to go out all the time," says Suze, a 38-year-old former bartender. "Even five years ago I felt compelled to hit bars and clubs a couple of nights a week just to see people. But now I'm pretty connected to everyone online. I talk to my ex on instant messenger, I've met dates on Craigslist, and I keep up with everyone's social life through Livejournal. I really only go out when there's a fun event going on."

While the appeal of Craigslist may never wane, since 2003 a new tool for wasting time online has surfaced. The overwhelming popularity of social networking sites like Friendster, Myspace, and Tribe.net has changed the way we flirt and hook up, perhaps permanently.

"The girl I am seeing isn't into e-mail or Friendster or Myspace or anything like that," says Morgan, a 40-year-old accountant for a wine distributor. "She's not really online at all, which seems weird to me. But she works in a salon so it just isn't part of her life. Since we haven't been able to do the usual getting to know you conversations over e-mail we talk on the phone a lot more. It was kind of awkward at first, but it's getting easier. It's just moving a lot more slowly than what I'm used to."

Friendster, which boasts 19 million profiles, started the trend. The Internet-addicted logged on in cities like Manhattan, San Diego, and San Francisco, but before long the entire country was Friendster friendly. "Dude, my dad is on Friendster," says Kate, a 24-year-old account manager. "He met his girlfriend there. I don't want him to look at my profile and see all the testimonials from my friends because he'll think I'm a drunk slut."

"Usually I see a girl somewhere and talk to her first, but I might use Friendster as a way to get to know her," says Carolina, a 29-year-old financial analyst for an LGBT website. "It isn't a dating site, so it's low pressure."

Friendster, which *New York* magazine described as "a high school dance mixed with a virtual Rolodex," allows users to connect with friends and friends of friends up to four degrees of separation, thus creating the sensation of community. Early on, the site grew so quickly that it often crashed, causing regular users to defect to other similar but newer sites like Myspace. com and Tribe.net. "They are all basically the same thing," says Forrest, a freelance graphic designer. "I switched to Myspace for a while but it's really dominated by fourteen-year-olds so I switched back to Friendster. Although the other day I was having dinner in a Mexican restaurant and three guys at the table next to me were having a conversation about which was gayer, Myspace or Friendster. They seemed to think Friendster was the gayest."

Like any cheap place to hang out and gossip, dykes have flocked to Friendster. "It's totally a drama-magnet," says Kelli, a buyer for a popular sex-toy store in Chicago. "Everyone is on Friendster—it almost functions like a bulletin board for the queer community. It's where all the parties get announced, and everyone promotes their drag performances and stuff on it." She pauses to sip the latte in front of her. "It's the testimonials that get you in trouble," she says, referring to one of Friendster's popular functions in which users can leave testimonials to each other that serve as records of relationships. The remarks may seem appropriate at the time, but it's a lot like leaving your journal open for everyone to read. "I left a testimonial to my then-girlfriend all about how in love we were. She kept complaining that I hadn't left one for her yet until I finally did it. And now I feel weird removing it, but I don't feel that way about her anymore and I don't want my current lady to see it.

"I was totally addicted to Myspace for a while," says Kelli. The problem was that everyone I knew was on it and they were all writing blogs about what they did the night before and leaving comments on each other's pages with inside jokes. And I was kind of stalking my ex. Well, not stalking her, but I was very interested in who she was sleeping with, so I was constantly combing everyone's blogs for mention of her and who she might be hooking up with. Finally it got so bad I just deleted my Myspace account so I couldn't look anymore. It was depressing me."

Friendster is a lot like a reality TV show about dyke drama that LOGO should produce. Everyone is hooking up, fighting, and breaking up all right there for the world to see. It's a little like bad lesbian porn," says Carolina.

but what about real porn?

The Internet is crawling with it—and it seems that in between sex and schadenfreude queer women are getting off online. "I look at porn online all the time," says Lauryn Pigeon, 28, a Brooklyn resident and sometime DJ. "But I really only like straight porn," she says. I never look at lesbian porn. I look at gangbang sites and interracial porn. So does Carolina," she says, referring to her best friend. "We have the same taste. Basically we're like Jewish butch lesbian frat boys."

"I never look at lesbian porn," says Ace, a 30-year-old financial consultant also from Brooklyn. "I look at mostly gay male and straight. I'm into anal sites and kink like spanking videos. I will pretty much look at anything as long as the players look like they are enjoying it. I've explored a lot of kink through the Internet, but it was all stuff I already knew I wasn't into, like blood sports and scat."

"I look at gay male porn. I don't look at lesbian porn because it doesn't represent the girls I go for. I like real-looking queer women in San Francisco and New York," says Nina, a 32-year-old receptionist for an advertising firm. When asked about porn sites that feature real queer women, like the Cyber-dyke network or Darkplay.net, she replies, "Never heard of them."

When asked if she uses online porn to explore fetishes and kink, she replies, "I prefer experimenting with partners. I might check something out on the web that I'm curious about, but if I'm into something, I want to explore it in person."

"I look at 89.com—it's a free site where you can look at snippets of videos that have come out recently," says Karen, a 30-year-old French teacher. "I only look at the gay part. There's like all these subsections like gay cowboy, gay Europe, and gay bondage. I also like to read smut stories on a site called Nifty. com. People post erotic stores, though my girlfriend says they aren't very good and she's right."

Karen says, "Most of the time I spend online is on instant messenger. My previous relationship was long distance and we spent a lot of time chatting online. We had tons of sex on instant messenger. And we sent each other dirty e-mails. My current girlfriend and I had sex over instant messenger a lot in the beginning." Karen and her girlfriend, Maya, share an office in the French department. "When we first got together, we couldn't stop touching each other. But we were afraid someone would walk in. Once we had instant-messenger sex while another teacher was actually in the office. We both sat there at our respective computers as if we were working."

"I have that conversation archived!" says Maya.

"Instant messaging allows me to be connected to everyone I know pretty much all the time," says Jules, a freelance writer from San Diego. Jules explains that she keeps in touch with lovers all over the world through instant messaging and e-mail. "I travel a lot, and I have a lot of play partners. We keep up with each other's lives through the Internet. It collapses the physical distance. I like to flirt over text messages as well. Sometimes I use text messages as a way to get a girl hot before we go on a date. I'll send her something about how I want to see her tied up so I know she has to think about it all day at work."

About half of the people I spoke to for this sidebar were interviewed over instant messenger. And everyone I chatted with agreed that it was a great tool for flirting—but also dangerous because without inflection and body language it's easy to misunderstand each other. "My girlfriend has outlawed instant-message conversations now because we fight too much," says Sal, a 38-year-old librarian from Seattle.

dating the web

But what about the all the dating sites out there? Isn't anyone using them to get girls? "I feel like dating sites aren't good for meeting people because there is too much pressure on the fact that you are dating. And you can really get a better sense of someone through a site like Myspace or Friendster because you see someone interact with their friends," explains Ace. "I've used Gay.com and PlanetOut Personals and had mixed results. But that's the same across the board as far as the Internet is concerned.

"When I first moved to the Bay Area from Seattle I used PlanetOut as a way to make new friends. I went on a few dates with girls I met, but nothing really turned into anything," says Sal.

"I met one of my good friends over PlanetOut Personals," explains Nina. "It wasn't a sexual thing. But I'm glad I met her. And I met a former girlfriend through PlanetOut. But I really prefer things that aren't designed as dating sites."

"The problem with a lot of the personals sites is that they aren't specific enough. I'm not just a woman seeking a woman—I'm a queer butch top seeking a submissive, kinky, femme bottom. And you don't get that kind of specificity with dating sites," explains Ace. "Butchfemmematchmaker.com seems better designed, but I checked it out recently and it didn't seem to have a lot of people on it. I've also looked at a lot of sites that claim to have millions of profiles of bisexual women and lesbians on them, but when you log on it's all porn pictures and people looking for sex with women but not what I consider dyke sex. I mean, they aren't dykes. Technically they are women who want to have sex with women, but they don't appeal to me," says Ace.

Recently I came across a site called executivelesbiandating. com and tried to sign up for it. They claim to have hundreds of thousands of executive lesbians looking for serious relationships. They charge you a large fee to sign up. It's designed to keep out the riffraff like myself. I filled out a profile and submitted it for approval but no one ever got back to me. "I don't really think they exist," says Carolina. "How could there be hundreds of thousands of lonely rich lesbians looking to get married? Why haven't I ever met one in person?"

social networking sites

Social networking sites have pretty much become virtual dyke bars. They're free, they allow you to spy on your ex, you can tell who's dating who by reading the comments people leave on each other's profiles, and they often include blogs filled with references to last night's activities. They basically meet your every lesbian need.

partial list of social network websites

360.YAHOO.COM: linked to Yahoo! IDs

43THINGS.COM: users are connected by similarities in lists they create.

ASMALLWORLD.COM: an invitation-only network

DOWNELINK.COM: LGBT community network

FACEBOOK.COM: college kids love this one

FACEPARTY.COM: sounds dirty, I know. But it's another college-oriented site

FAVORVILLE.COM: people helping people

FRIENDSTER.COM: the oldest and largest of the social sites

GREATESTJOURNAL.COM: online journaling and community

LINKEDIN.COM: for the suit set

LIVEJOURNAL.COM: online journaling and community

MYSPACE.COM: even Paris Hilton has a Myspace profile

NEXOPIA.COM: Canadians like this one

ORKUT.COM: Google's version of the social network

PASSADO.COM: social and business together

QUEPASA.COM: Latino-oriented network

SLIDE.COM: share your photos and make friends

SMS.AC: keep in touch with your mobile phone

TRIBE.NET: another big one like Friendster and Myspace

IWIW.COM: invite-only

WAYN.COM: travelers

XANGA.COM: blogs and networking

XUQA.COM: college networking site, similar to Facebook

safety first!

There are some safety rules to follow for meeting girls online.

Use common sense. Don't agree to meet someone you don't have a good feeling about. If you feel nervous about their level of honesty, go with that. Not everyone online is what they present themselves to be.

Be wary of anyone who insists on meeting immediately. It's best to exchange several e-mails and have a phone conversation before agreeing to meet. You can get a good sense of someone by talking to them on the phone. E-mail is too impersonal and lacks intonation, but over the phone you can listen to verbal cues.

Don't let yourself get pushed into anything you don't feel comfortable with. If someone makes demands of you before you've met, be suspicious.

Always arrange to meet someone for the first time in a public place. Let your friends know where you will be and what time to expect you home.

It's perfectly acceptable to end a date if the person turns out to be not what you expected. Simply explain that you don't think there's any chemistry between the two of you and then make a polite exit.

Google them. Google knows all. You can find out ridiculous amounts of information by Googling someone's full name. Don't worry, it's not stalking. Googling someone before you meet them is a basic safety precaution.

CHAPTER 5

flirting for dummies

FLIRTING IS AN essential tool for getting dates. If you don't know how to flirt, sister, read up, because everyone needs to know how to flirt. Flirting is like social lubricant: It makes everything run smoother. Flirting is how you get people to do things for you, to notice you, and to like you. Flirting with people makes them feel good. Flirting gets you attention, dates, lovers, fuck buddies, and anything else you need.

how to flirt

Flatter the object of your attention. Compliment her appearance, her intelligence, her singing voice, whatever it is you notice about her.

A long slow glance and a sweet smile will get someone's attention. But don't ogle them—you'll seem like a perv.

Your body language is very important. Leaning in toward someone with open arms says, "I like you." Arms across your chest and facing away from someone says, "Stay away."

Have good grooming. Being well groomed gives you confidence and helps you to project attractiveness.

Don't be afraid to talk to women. Approach them with confidence and ask to buy them a drink, dance with you, join you at your table, or whatever.

Listen to her as she speaks. Ask her questions about herself.

making conversation

Are you a little awkward when it comes to starting conversations? Do you dread making small talk? Small talk isn't really all that bad once you get the hang of it. And it's a great door opener. It helps you make connections, meet people, get dates, network, and improve your social life.

IN THE HOOD

Sick of walking past that hot girl from the gym every day on the way home from work? Well, don't just walk by pretending not to notice her. Stop and say hi. She's probably just as shy as you are and will welcome the introduction.

Things to say:

"Hey you work out at my gym, don't you?"

"Do you live on this street? I see you around pretty often."

"Do you know where there's a mail box (or post office, gas station, medical marijuana seller)?"

"Hi, I forgot your name but I think we met at (insert club or sex party here)."

"Hey, I like your T-shirt."

"Hi, how are you?"

"Your hair looks good."

"Do you think it's going to rain?"

other places to start a conversation

THE BOOKSTORE

You are browsing the new releases section when suddenly you see this hot tattooed babe flipping through the collected works of Tom of Finland. Quick, what do you say?

"I love his work. Have you seen (insert name of a similar artist here)?"

"Oh, I own that book. It's wonderful."

"What's that you are looking at? It seems interesting."

THE GROCERY STORE

You are shopping for Lean Cuisine and Meals for One when you spot a shaggy-haired cutie in the produce aisle. What do you say?

"Do you have any idea how to cook eggplant?"

"Do you know where the wine aisle is?"

"You look familiar—have we met before?"

THE BAR

There she is at the jukebox, the chickie you've been admiring all evening. Your beer is nearly empty, so you cross the room in her direction. What do you say?

"What are you going to play?"

"Hi, my name is…"

"Can I buy you a beer?"

True story: My best friend moved to San Francisco from Boston when she was 23. For a while she was pretty shy and didn't hook up with girls much. We used to hit all of San Francisco's sceney dyke places together, but mostly we'd just dance and drink. But after a few weeks every time I went to some lezzer dance club with her she spent half the night snogging with some tramp in the corner. I asked her what was going on and she told me that she'd finally figured out that girls wanted to make out with someone or they wouldn't be there, but they were pretty much standing around waiting for someone else to make a move. And from that point on she was a stud. If no one ever got up the nerve to make the first move, no one would ever get laid.

getting dates

OK, SO YOU'VE found someone you want to go out with. Maybe you met her or him online, maybe you cruised her in the women's restroom at the mall. Wherever you found her she's cool and now you want to do that thing that lesbians have such a hard time with, you know, *go on a date.*

so how do you make this happen? make the (gasp!) first move

WELL, FIRST OF all, depending on how you met, you'll probably want to ask for her phone number. Even if you've been chatting online or over e-mail, you'll want to arrange your date over the phone to avoid confusion and mix-ups.

One of the things that I hear ladies talking about the most is how both parties are afraid to be the aggressor. We were all raised with, um, let's see—zero vocabulary for initiating sex. In fact for the most part I'd say that those of us raised female were probably taught that the only way to get dates is to flirt and be coy and hope someone comes along and demands that you go out with them. I'm sure there are plenty of swaggering butches reading this thinking, "What? I know how to ask a lady out." And if that's you, just skip over this next part and read up on underwear choices or something.

asking someone out

The first step in going on a date is to make sure you both know you are going on a date. If you want to take someone out, say so. And don't use willy-nilly phrases like "we should hang out" or "let's have coffee." Just say you would like to take her out on a date. It's not hard. If it feels really foreign, practice a few times in the mirror at home.

the pre-date

The pre-date date is usually reserved for people you meet online. If you meet in person, you probably already know you are attracted to each other and share some chemistry. But meeting online is slightly riskier. You can find someone incredibly charming in e-mail, talk on the phone for hours and hours, and have everything in common—but still not click in person. So arrange a pre-date in order to meet in person and ascertain whether or not you'd like to go out on an actual date. Pre-dates should be short and easy. Coffee is always a good option, so is a drink, or maybe a walk in the park. Dinner implies you'll be spending the evening together and could get dicey if you aren't interested. Keep it low-key. The goal of a pre-date is to spend an hour or so talking and hanging out and getting to know the person. If you are attracted to each other, you can ask her out at that time. Initiate a pre-date by saying something along the lines of "I'd like to meet you in person— can we have coffee sometime?"

If you meet someone for a pre-date and you find that you don't click, excuse yourself as soon as possible. Have your coffee or whisky sour and then say, "It was nice meeting you. I don't think we're right for dating, but take care."

invite her over for a home-cooked meal

THE WAY TO her heart is through her stomach. Everyone knows this. Cooking for your date is romantic, fun, impressive—and it will make her swoon. Don't worry about being a good cook. I've got two fool-proof recipes for you. Both look extremely impressive but are actually easy and nearly impossible to screw up.

The first recipe is for roast chicken. Pulling an entire bird out of the oven, all nicely browned and crispy, is going to make you seem like Suzy Homemaker. The second recipe is for stuffed squash, in case she's a vegetarian.

You don't need much to round either of these recipes out into a meal. Just serve either recipe with a large green salad, a bottle of wine, and a loaf of good French bread.

Set the table beautifully, light some candles, put on some music and you've got all the makings for a romantic evening.

Roast Chicken

1 three-to-five-pound chicken
Olive oil, salt and pepper, an onion
Shallow baking dish or cast iron pan
Other possible things to season it with: some sprigs of rosemary or a cut-up lemon to put in the body cavity are nice but not necessary.

1. Preheat the oven to 400.
2. Remove the liver and other weird stuff from the body cavity. (I always boil these for the cat—if you don't have a cat, just throw them out. Or boil them to make broth for gravy, if you want gravy, that is.)
3. Rinse the chicken inside and out, and then dry it off with paper towels. Rub a little olive oil on it and then sprinkle lots of salt and pepper all over it inside and out. Lots of salt. Cut the onion into quarters, break it up, and put it in the bottom of the pan. This is so the skin doesn't stick to the bottom of the pan.
4. Put the chicken breast-side down in the pan and put it in the oven.
5. Roast it for 20 minutes per pound of body weight. When it's done, the juices will run clear after you stick it with a fork.
6. Let the bird sit for about 10 minutes after you take it out of the oven. Then pull on the leg joint and the leg and thigh should separate from the body. Cut the

joint with a sharp knife. Do the same on the other side. Then flip it over and cut the breasts away from the bone. Save the body for soup.

Stuffed Acorn Squash

1 large acorn squash
1 cup brown rice
2 cups sliced mushrooms, either plain old white or brown mushrooms. Or use fancy porcini mushrooms if you see them.
2 cups chicken broth (if you are making this for a vegetarian, just use water instead)
A little bit of Parmesan or other strong, aged cheese

1. Preheat the oven to 350.
2. Cook the brown rice with the mushrooms and chicken broth.
3. While the rice is cooking, cut the acorn squash in half and put the two halves cut-side down in a baking dish with a little water in the bottom.
4. Roast it for 45 minutes or until it's soft.
5. Take the squash out of the oven and let it cool slightly. Scoop out the flesh and mix it with the cooked brown rice and mushroom combo. Add a little Parmesan cheese to bind it. Salt and pepper to taste.
6. Pile the squash-rice-mushroom mixture back into the squash shell. Put a few slices of Parmesan cheese on top and brown it under the broiler until it's bubbly.

more date ideas

One of the scariest things about asking people out on dates is figuring out what the hell to do with them after they say yes. It's easy though to charm someone's pants off if you have a charmed evening.

The following suggestions for fun dates are tried and true. While on tour recently, I asked dykes from all over the U.S. to tell me about their favorite date activities. All the dates below ended with hot monkey sex, and some even led to falling in love.

"I took my date to an erotica reading. We got all turned on listening to the stories, but it was our first date and we didn't know each other well enough to just go home and have sex. So instead we had a cocktail and then went for a walk around a nearby park. I was dying because I wanted to kiss her, but I felt like I needed to wait until the end of the night. Around 2 a.m. we decided to get some food so we stopped at a café and had potato pancakes and coffee. All through dinner she kept looking at me like she wanted me to kiss her and this made me feel more bold and aggressive. After we finished eating she told me she was really attracted to me and wanted to know if I would come home with her. I couldn't believe it. We grabbed a cab to her place and made out in the back seat the whole way home. That erotica reading really did the trick."

"I like to treat my girlfriend to dinner dates. I dress up in something sexy, usually lingerie, and cook her dinner. Sometimes I will get really elaborate and plan out an entire evening around the outfit I want to wear. I like to pour her a scotch and let her watch porn while I do the cooking."

"I like it when girls invite me over to do something dorky like watch TV or play video games. It's so much more comfortable than going out on some formal date."

"My most romantic date ever involved making dinner for someone I was really hot for. It was our second date but we'd had sex on our first so this was kind of the getting-to-know-you date.

I invited her to my house to watch a very interesting but totally nonnarrative experimental film I'd been wanting to see. Instead of cooking something elaborate I made a big platter of finger foods, things like cut-up vegetables, cheeses, bread, salami, and olives. It was perfect because it was more like snacks than dinner and we ate while we watched the movie. We had wine and sat on the floor next to each other. At first we tried very hard to pay attention to what was going on in the film but eventually we both admitted we were more interested in each other than we were in the movie. She leaned over and kissed me and we made out for hours on the floor in front of the television. She spent the night and in the morning we both agreed that the entire night had been charmed."

"I like taking girls out for cupcakes. Usually they really appreciate being treated to something more special and fun than dinner in some boring restaurant."

"For my birthday my girlfriend planned out a whole evening of romantic events. First she took me to her favorite Italian restaurant for an early dinner. The waiters all knew her there and she did all the ordering, which made it seem extra special. Then we had coffee at a café nearby. Then she rushed me off on the back of her motorcycle without telling me where she was going. We took a long scenic ride out to the beach and got there just in time to watch the sun set into the water. We stood there kissing until the sun was completely gone. Then we drove home and had wild sex all night."

"I like dates to movies. Sitting next to each other is so intense because you are almost touching and will accidentally brush your arms against each other but you never know if it's on purpose or not. I usually try to hold my date's hand at some point in the movie and that sets the precedent to holding hands once we leave."

"I always take my dates to the diviest bars I can find. I like being in seedy, dark places with a person I'm attracted to. It makes the whole date seem more sexually charged."

"My hottest date ever was when this photographer took me on a tour of Open Studios, this biannual event where all the artists in the city open their studios to the public so you can come in and see their work. She was a well-connected photographer so she knew tons of people and introduced me to everyone. It made the day seem extra special. After she suggested we unwind at a Japanese bathhouse so we ended up being naked with each other within the first few hours of meeting. It was very sexy."

"I was seeing this girl who was really into being tied up and she told me she wanted to go to a sex party. We'd only gone on a few dates but I took her to a sex party and tied her up while people watched. At first I was skeptical because we hadn't known each other long and that seemed like an intense activity for a third date, but in the end it was so hot that it forced us to get to know each other and become more intimate really quickly."

"My date took me to a screening of a porno film she was in. She didn't bother telling me she was in the porno, she just waited until her scene came on and watched me go into shock."

"A cute butch girl asked me out recently and I planned out a really elaborate evening. I had a car pick us up and take us to a really abandoned part of town down by the water. I took her through several dark alleyways and around ramshackle warehouses and through all sorts of intimidating dark spaces. We walked for a long time and I pretended I didn't have a location in mind. It was very scenic and creepy and deserted, but also romantic. She was really nervous because she thought for sure we were lost. Eventually we arrived at an old dingy bar, the heart of my plan. We drank whisky and talked about our lives. Then at nine the car reappeared as if by magic and whisked us away to a fancy restaurant where we ate mussels and scallops and delicious French bread. At the end of the evening we took a taxi to my place and spent the night in each other's arms."

"I took a date to go see Karen Finley. It was fantastic. We saw her at a small theater and sat right up front. It felt really exciting and it made us bond."

"My favorite date ever was when someone I really liked took me to see Diamanda Galas for Halloween."

"I love picnic dates. Usually I'll pack a delicious picnic and take my date to the park. We'll spread everything out on a big blanket and spend the afternoon lying in the grass looking at the clouds. It's so romantic."

"I took a girl I was seeing to Golden Gate Park for the day. We drove paddle boats around the lake and shared soft-serve cones afterward. It was very fun and sweet and romantic and really helped us feel comfortable around each other."

"Recently someone took me to a comics convention. We met a lot of female artists and she bought me a signed illustration. It was a lot of fun."

"I took a girl I really liked to the Natural History Museum. There was an exhibit on endangered species and she got really upset and spent the whole day crying. But it worked out in the end because I comforted her and she ended up falling in love with me."

"My favorite dates are when people ask me out for activities like bike riding or rollerblading. I like having something physical to do together."

"My date took me to the Museum of Modern Art to see an exhibit on graphic design. I'm a graphic designer and I really appreciated her thoughtfulness. After the exhibit we went for a walk and had a cappuccino at a nearby café. It was an afternoon date and neither of us wanted it to end so we each kept ordering coffee after coffee. Finally when it was nearly time for dinner she asked if I was hungry. We had dinner and drank wine and really enjoyed each other's company. At the end of the night she kissed me and I thought I was going to die. But she wouldn't come home with me. She said she really liked me and wanted to be friends before we fucked. She's my girlfriend now."

"My last date played softball and she invited me to come watch her tournament. It was fun to see her so excited about something. I got all turned on watching her play sports and we had amazing sex in a hotel room that night."

"I took a girl to a sex party for our first date. I bent her over a table and spanked her, and then I offered the paddle to anyone who wanted to use it. She ended up getting spanked by two big butches for a really long time. They got her so worked up that she begged me to have sex with her. It was definitely a great night."

"I took a girl out for dessert and champagne and spoon-fed her the crème brulée. She was putty. She went home with me that night."

"I like it when dates want to go on long walks together. Anywhere is fine, even just around the city. And then when the sexual tension gets really high, I like to make out in doorways and on street corners."

"This trannyboy I was going out with took me to a workshop on female dominance. I asked him if he was trying to tell me something and he just smiled. I learned a lot at the workshop and put it to good use later that night."

"I like formal dates. I want to pick a girl up at her place and have her make me wait while she finishes her makeup. It always heightens the sexiness of the date if she makes me wait in the living room for a few minutes while she puts on lipstick or whatever girls do. I usually bring flowers. And I like to open the doors for her and help her out of the car. Especially if she's wearing a dress and heels. I like taking girls to romantic restaurants and ordering for them and making them feel special and adored."

CHAPTER 6

dating protocol

I AM ALWAYS shocked at the number of people who don't know the proper way to prepare for a date. Granted, it's tricky. No one wants to take the risk of seeming overeager or overdressed, and in general downplaying expectations by not putting too much pressure on a first date can quell your anxiety as well as your date's. But there are still a few things that simply must not be overlooked.

let's talk grooming

NO ONE WANTS to date a grungy, unwashed lesbian. I don't care how cool your aesthetic is. I don't care if you are totally immersed in some kind of dirty-ass dyke subculture where looking like you just rolled out of a dumpster is the hippest thing. If you are unwashed no one wants to go out with you. So bathe before your date. And I don't mean in the morning before work. A date, especially first date, deserves a grooming ritual all its own.

how you smell

We all know how lesbians are with the chemical-sensitivity thing so you may want to take that into consideration before you get all tarted up with perfume and cologne. As a high femme, I like perfume and I appreciate a butch who tells me she likes the way I smell. Nothing makes me swoon faster than having someone murmur that they like they way I smell while they are kissing my neck. But unfortunately not all lesbos get into it. In fact I dated someone for several years who would wrinkle her nose as if something was rotten in the refrigerator whenever I put on any scent. I got so used to not wearing any that it took me a couple of years to get back into the groove.

So, no overdoing it with the cologne or perfume. No one wants a smelly date.

If you do wear scent, someone should really have to be all up in your grill before they can smell it. If it trails behind you as you cross the room, tone it down a bit.

how are your nails?

Hands are the first thing your date will notice about you. They should be clean, with nails trimmed very short and filed down. Nip any hangnails and rub some moisturizer into your cuticles.

If you are femme and your nails are normally done, make sure you have a fresh manicure with a nice clean unchipped coat of polish. The sexiest femme nail is very short, filed into a smooth round shape, and painted a bold color, indicating both an interest in feminine grooming rituals but also a willingness, desire, and ability to please a lover. No offense to my acrylic-sporting sisters. I understand a diva needs her claws. And many butch dykes appreciate a confirmed pillow queen. But for most of us the short nail is the way to go.

Listen to me when I say that all those alternative femme manicures like the one hand long, one short, or the short nails on the index and pointer finger only are just plain tacky. Like the femme version of wearing a buzz cut with a tail. Not only that, but what if your lady wants more than two fingers? Just keep your nails short, ladies.

dress nicely for your date

NO SKANKY, DIRTY jeans and ripped T-shirts unless that's your aesthetic and you've raised the look to an art. Don't do the whole "I don't want to look too eager so I'm going to dress down" thing. You'll just feel underdressed when your date shows up in a suit or a skirt and heels. Dressing up is a way of showing respect for the person who wants to take you out.

what about the details?

How is your hair? Is it clean, styled, not overloaded with so much product it looks difficult to touch? That's good. What about your breath? Do a quick breath check and keep some gum or mints handy. Bad breath is the biggest turn off out there. Just the other night I was approached in a club by a positively dreamy girl. She was to die for, very androgynous, European accent, worked in the fashion industry, extremely charming. But her breath nearly melted my eyebrows and I had to make a quick exit.

what not to wear

In addition to dressing up for your date, you may also want to consider keeping some of your more outrageous outfits in the closet until you've felt each other out a little bit. Don't wear anything too slutty. If you are walking down the street and someone asks you if you are "working," chances are you've gone overboard with the sexy look. Femme sisters, listen up. I learned this the hard way.

Don't wear anything too crude or ridiculous. Save your "Ask me about my penis" T-shirt for another time. Same goes for the "I heart my clit" T-shirt. I'm sure your genitals are nice, but forcing someone you just met to think about them is nonconsensual. Don't wear a whole bunch of weird-ass Gay Pride crap, either. You are about to go on a date with another woman; she already knows you are gay, so you can just put that rainbow-cat sweatshirt back in the drawer.

Other things not to wear on a first date include pants so tight people can tell what kind of pubic hairdo you are sporting. Nothing extremely low cut. If your date can't seem to look you in the eye, you might be showing too much cleavage. Don't wear jeans that show your butt crack. And don't wear anything weird or loud or ill-fitting. Also, you may be enamored of those extremely high vintage heels, but they should remain at home until you've had a few dates and you are sure you won't have to do tons of walking. Wearing risky shoes on a first date is just going to be a big bummer when you don't feel like dancing because your feet hurt.

date fashion

20 questions with queer and dirty fashion designer Parisa Parnian of Rigged Out/Fitters.

Rigged Out/Fitters was formed in 2005 by a glamorous queer Persian dyke named Parisa Parnian. Parisa is striking, five foot eight and very curvy. She's powerful and sexy, and dresses very feminine but with an aggressive edge. She looks a bit like something out of Tennessee Williams with a little Leather Tuscadero thrown in. I found her in her home office surrounded by snappily dressed houseboys, one of whom served us martinis while we talked.

You have some pretty strong ideas about fashion, and your clothing line is really about adorning

butches. **Usually we think of boyish or andro queers being less decorated than femmes. We think of them as dressing down to defeminize themselves. But that isn't your vision.**

PARISA: I like dandy boys. I like boys and girls who look rugged and butch with a vintage sense of style. I like it when boys have a sense of fashion and can appreciate the history of the looks they are pulling together. I like boys that aren't afraid to be fashionable. I like my dates to look like they put time into their appearance.

You like metrosexuals, don't you?

PARISA: No, not exactly. I don't want to date a boy that is so narcissistic that they are more interested in how they look when we go out than being able to mutually appreciate each other's sense of style. I like it when my date dresses up for the occasion. I like to see that someone has put some time into his outfit. I like to smell cologne on people. I don't want them to go overboard. I mean, if we're just taking a stroll together, they don't need to be wearing a suit. But I want him or her to dress appropriately for the occasion.

How do you feel about a good old shirt and tie? It's a basic but it usually works. I like girls in ties.

PARISA: A shirt and tie seems formulaic to me. I prefer it when my date shows off his or her personal style. Even if they put on something classic like a cowboy shirt and jeans, I want to see the outfit pulled together with a belt buckle that expresses her personality. Something unique. That really excites me. Even a T-shirt and jeans can be sexy if it's a very carefully put-together combination. I don't like it when it looks as if someone has dressed color by numbers. A dyke's imagination and personality should show through.

Yeah, I know what you mean. My ex was great at putting together the carefully selected T-shirt and jeans. She put so much effort into her outfits. It's not like she dressed up; her style was all about jeans and vintage football jerseys. But she put a lot of time into picking out her clothes. Her jeans were always designer, and her T-shirts were always very carefully thrifted. She was obsessed with belt buckles and had a huge collection of them. She got them at antique stores or off eBay.

PARISA: That's very hot. When a butch woman puts effort into putting her outfit together, it's very sexy. The biggest mistake butches can make is trying to hide their bodies under baggy clothes. Especially big women. Their bigness is what's hot about them, and if they hide that under a sweatshirt that's five sizes too big, they just look like shapeless lumps.

Yeah, I agree. Butch bodies are hot. I want to see an actual body under all those layers. And it's not that wearing a mountain of clothes will make you look smaller. It just makes you look like Grimace.

PARISA: Yes, clothes should be body conscious. We're queers and we have a different standard of beauty than straight people. A big body seems powerful and sexy.

Is there anything else you expect from your date fashion-wise?

PARISA: Well, I expect her to not be wearing girl underwear.

True dat.

PARISA: And I expect her to put as much time into her appearance as I put into mine. It's not all about me trying to impress her. She should also be trying to impress me.

Absolutely. OK, let's talk hair. What do you think is a good choice for butch hairstyles?

PARISA: A buzz cut is a turn off, it's too much of a default. Though it does work on some boys. Often if a boy has a very pretty face, having very fashionable hair will make her look too feminine. A buzz cut works in that case because it's defeminizing.

I've seen the boys you are attracted to. They all have shaggy stylish hair.

PARISA: Yes, I like the shaggy-haired emo boy look. I love it when boys have a lock of hair falling into their eyes. It makes me want to bitch-slap them. But there's no one set haircut that fits every personality or aesthetic. A dyke's haircut should flatter her own personal aesthetic.

But anyone sporting a mullet should seriously reconsider it. I know that they've come back in a really stylish form, and I'm all for it. But that old-school mullet? The "business in the front, party in the back" look is the one I'm talking about.

PARISA: I had that hairstyle for a while. I was wearing it in New York where it was totally fashionable and ironic. But I went to Arizona for a visit and nearly got gay-bashed by some rednecks in a pickup truck.

Do you think we use hair as a way of indicating our sexual desires?

PARISA: Absolutely. For instance, I think a lot of femmes cut off their hair when they first come out so that no one will question their sexuality.

Right. Because when you first come out, you don't really know about gender presentation or signifying sexual desire through your look. At that point you only care that straight people see you as queer and queers see you as queer. You don't really know if you want to be a femme princess, a butch top daddy, a wanderin' boi, a divine andro, or a sporty dyke. You don't know about all the different ways there are to be queer.

PARISA: Exactly. And sometimes we associate certain things with certain styles but it turns out we're wrong. When I had a short pompadour everyone thought I was a butch top daddy.

You are a butch top daddy in a high femme body.

PARISA: Yes, but that's a secret!

Do you like long-haired butch girls?

PARISA: I like any girl who pays attention to her appearance and has her own personal style. It doesn't really matter what length her hair is.

So what about yourself? What do you like to wear on a date?

PARISA: It really depends on who I'm going out with. I don't have a default aesthetic. I would probably consider my date and what my energy feels like in relation to them. I went on a date the other day with someone who I'd pegged as a submissive young boy. And I knew that she had asked me out expecting me to be the older woman, the teacher. This inspired me to wear a wool skirt. It was A line and plaid and hit at the knee. I wore it with knee-high boots and a jacket. But I hoochied it up with a little eighties ho-bag drop-neck camisole under the jacket. It's good to have one piece that surprises people.

So are you indicating a sexual proclivity with your look?

PARISA: I think that's part of the role of fashion, indicating your sexual proclivities. Though the difference between the New York fashion scene and the fashion scene in other queer communities across the country is that people in New York are more interested in looking like individuals. Fashion indicates more than just how much sex you are having.

In San Francisco people do a lot of default butch-femme. The femme wears a corset, heels, fishnets, and maybe a feather boa. Femme is very performed. The butch wears jeans, a wallet chain, a work shirt, a buzz cut. People in San Francisco have a very strong queer aesthetic, but it's not as advanced as New York. But I still find it very sexy.

PARISA: Corsets, leopard print, feather boas, fishnets. These things have been around since the early twentieth century. They are all about classic glamour. But I would feel like a copout if I wore that outfit.

Over the years when I have decided to camp it up as a femme, I have gone out of my way to avoid that look. But that classic femme look indicates a certain sensibility. A sexually available sensibility.

It's naughty, don't you think? And it's reminiscent of femme-fatale movie stars, Rita Hayworth, Lana Turner. It doesn't work on me. I feel like I'm playing dress up.

PARISA: It's an intimidating look. It says, "I'm all woman, so stay away unless you can handle me." Girls who dress down a bit are more approachable and probably get hit on more. But who wants to make it easy?

Good point. What are you inspired by right now?

PARISA: I'm really into the idea of the sultry gypsy girl and the queer sailor boy. Like in *Querelle*.

And what kind of sexual proclivity is that indicating?

PARISA: A queer and dirty one, of course.

punctuality is hot

For Goddess's sake, don't arrive late. It's lame and indicates you don't really care about your date's time. We all know about gay time, it's like Hawaii time, about two hours later than the mainland. But don't set a date for 7 p.m. and then arrive at 7 p.m. gay time. Arriving on time shows you are responsible and are taking your date seriously. Your date will be impressed and much more comfortable with you if she feels like you care about her. And the more comfortable she is the more likely she is to make out with you.

what to bring

Bringing a small gift for your date is a really nice gesture and will make her feel special. Flowers, maybe a bottle of wine if she drinks, some candy, stationery, really anything small and inexpensive is appropriate. Don't go buying anything expensive—this will just make you look like a desperate loony. But a small token of affection is always welcome.

don't be boring!

Do you have trouble making small talk? If you are nervous or in general aren't much of a small-talk fan, brush up on current events before your date. Read a newspaper, read *The Nation*, read The Huffington Post. Read all the *New York Times* headlines. Read reviews of current movies and books. Arm yourself with pop culture info and you'll have lots of stuff to fall back on should the conversation stall during your evening.

What does your date do for a living? Ask her about her work and listen attentively so you can ask questions. If she has a hobby or an art, encourage her to tell you all about it. Most people like to talk about themselves. With a little encouragement you can get her to open up and you'll learn lots about her.

who pays?

LESBIANS HAVE THEIR share of gender roles and preconceived notions about who does what for whom and to whom and all that stuff. But they really don't apply when it comes to who picks up the check. Butches often feel as if they are expected to pay because they are assuming a more masculine role. And femmes get confused and don't know if they should insist or not. And what about femme-femme dates or butch-butch ones? Or any other date where there is no obvious masculine-feminine dynamic?

Well, I'll put these questions to rest right now. If this is a first date, the person who did the asking does the paying. If someone treats you to dinner or a movie or whatever your first date activity is, offer to pay for something small after dinner like coffee or dessert.

If you've been on a few dates, it's time to start switching up the paying. If you can avoid it, don't go Dutch. It's tacky and a turn-off and makes you look cheap. Especially on a first date, you want your date to feel romantic and swept away by your charm. Picking up the tab makes you look suave. If you are being treated to dinner, thank your date sincerely and graciously accept her offer to treat you. If you feel a little unsure and don't want to be presumptuous, pull out your wallet when the check comes, and provided she's not a cad, she'll tell you to put it away and pay the bill herself.

After the first date, start alternating responsibility for the check. If you were treated the first time, then insist it's your turn the next time you go out. If you do it this way, you both get to enjoy the experience of being treated.

If you are femme and going on a date with an old-school butch, she will probably want to pay for dinner. Go ahead and let her—she likes picking up the tab and treating ladies to dinner. It's part of butch-femme dynamics. If she won't let you pay, insist she comes over to your place so you can cook dinner for her. She'll fall right in love.

money changes everything

Do things change if one of you makes more?

I'm sitting at the extremely fancy new neighborhood coffee shop that I've been writing in lately when my friend Stan tells me he only wants to date guys with money from now on. I set down my cup of free-trade organic coffee and ask, "What do you mean 'with money?' Do you want to date someone who will pay for everything, or do you just want to date someone who isn't as broke as we are."

"I want to date someone who wants to do bougie things and pay for them," he replies confidently. "I want to get treated to fancy restaurants more before I'm too old to be a dinner whore."

"What about egalitarianism? What about having your own power in a relationship?" I say. And Stan rolls his eyes at me and mutters, "Lesbians."

Fast-forward a month and I'm flipping through the stack of *Dwell* magazines on my date's coffee table. She's in the kitchen opening a bottle of wine when I'm suddenly struck by how expensive everything in her apartment clearly is. I hadn't noticed it until this, our third date, but I'm definitely dating someone who makes considerably more money than I do. I immediately feel like a loser. I look down at my Steve Madden shoes and think I should have worn the Charles Davids. Is she going to judge me? If she pays for everything, will I have to put out? Twenty minutes earlier I was fine. Now I'm a neurotic mess. I sneak my cellphone out of my handbag while she's in the kitchen and text Stan, "I think Suzanne makes a lot of money."

And in return I get a smiley face.

From the kitchen Suzanne calls out, "The cleaning lady doesn't come till Thursday so things are a bit of a wreck."

I text Stan, "OMG! She has a cleaning lady!"

"Maybe you should date her cleaning lady," Stan responds.

It's not that I'm afraid of money. I'd certainly like

more of it myself. But as a freelance writer I'm used to being very self-sufficient. Dating someone who makes radically more screws up my sense of equilibrium. I'm afraid the balance of power swings in their favor. Or I'll feel like I need to keep up, and I'm not sure what's worse.

My friend Lisa is seeing a woman who makes tons of money. Her girlfriend has very expensive taste and I've noticed that suddenly Lisa does, too. I don't know where she is getting the cash to go out every night. But I know the highly paid girlfriend isn't doing all the paying. I think Lisa would rather live beyond her means than admit that she can't afford the things her lady wants to do.

"I am not used to hanging out with people who make a lot of money," says Dana, a 30ish financial analyst dating in a land of ladies with coffee shop gigs. "So I basically just pay for everything. I like treating."

But there's a fine line between picking up the check because you like treating and paying because you want to be the one in charge. If someone does all the paying, does that mean they have expectations?

"My ex-girlfriend really resented the fact that I had more. She was so broke all the time. If we did anything I had to pay. And when we broke up, I felt very used," adds Val, a 30-something who routinely dates girls with less money than her.

"I've definitely dated girls who expected me to pay for everything because I make more," agrees Dana. "On first dates I'll choose somewhere cheap so my date can split the check with me. I don't want to set up expectations. Also, I think it's important to not pay for things until you have had sex."

"Most of the time I think the income gap works out for both parties. If you are the poorer one, you get a sugar momma. And if you have the money, your partner is eating out of the palm of your hand," says Val.

"You worry too much about this stuff," says Laura, an account manager with a modest income. Recently Laura went on a date with a model. "I thought she was just some tall, skinny girl when she asked me out. I didn't realize she was loaded till she picked me up in a limo."

"But you slept with her at the end of your date, didn't you?" I remind her.

"Well, yeah, I thought she was going to drop me off, but at the end of the night she asked if she could use my bathroom. And when she came out she was naked."

"So you slept with her because she spent so much money on you, right?"

"No," said Laura, "I just wanted to do it with a model."

getting a second date

IF EVERYTHING WENT well on your date and you want to see her again, say so before you part ways for the evening. Don't just say goodbye and leave her hanging wondering if and when you will call again, or if she should call you, or if you think she's too old, too fat, too young, too ugly, too lazy, or any of the other things that are probably going to run through her head if you don't say right away that you want to see her again.

You don't have to make a plan right then and there, but saying that you enjoyed yourself and you'd like to see her again will let her know you like her company. It's appropriate for either party to send an e-mail or text message the next morning thanking the other person for a nice time. Calling is good, too, but can sometimes feel like too much pressure if you call the very next day. Call when you are ready to make plans to see the person again, chat on the phone a bit, and ask her questions about herself and use the phone call to get to know each other a little better. Don't engage in a long, intimate conversation because usually after a really great date the lesbian "urge to merge" is on high and you need to be careful about taking things one step at a time.

The rule of thumb that most people follow for when to call is the "two-day rule." Waiting two days to call shows that you want to go slow, it allows the other person to relax knowing that you aren't scarily eager, and if you are dying to talk sooner, the anticipation will build and make your second date extra hot.

telling someone you aren't interested

What if you aren't interested in going out again? Well, if you've made it through a whole evening with the person and you are completely sure you don't want to see them again, thank them for a nice time, shake hands and say something along the lines of "I had fun hanging out with you, but I don't think we are right for dating. Maybe we should just be friends." Don't say you will call and then not call. That's bad behavior and will give you bad karma.

what if she doesn't call back?

Have you called someone after what you thought was a great date and then been disappointed when she didn't call you back? I know this can be really frustrating, but not returning someone's call reflects poorly on the person who doesn't return the call more than the person who does the calling.

She could have any number of reasons for not calling. Maybe her ex begged her to come back. Maybe she has an STD. Maybe you came on too strong and she got scared. Maybe she's flaky. Maybe she's scared. Maybe she's looking for someone more femme or butch. Maybe she's a jerk.

If you really thought the date went well and you are bewildered that she hasn't returned your call, then it's acceptable to call one more time and say something along the lines of "Hi, I really thought we had a nice time together. I haven't heard from you and I wanted to make sure you got my message. Let me know if you'd like to get together again." If you don't hear from her after your second message, let it go.

don't stress it

Meeting someone new can bring up all sorts of crazy, excited emotions. Don't let yourself get carried away with fantasies about what you are going to wear to your wedding. In the beginning before we know someone well, it's easy to start projecting our image of the "perfect" date onto them. But the truth is you know very little about her and she may turn out to be a huge disappointment. Save your excitement until you have had a few dates.

CHAPTER 7

sex, sex, sex

WELL, WHAT ELSE is dating about than having sex? Part of being a queer is being hot for another woman. But what do you do with her once you get her home? There are lots of ways to have queer sex. Queer sex is as varied as queer fashion, gender, and everything else. But there are few pointers that can help make your sex life hot and exciting, regardless of what you are doing between the sheets.

your mise en scène

If you are actively dating, you are probably actively having lovers and possibly bringing them home. So you want to make sure your bachelor pad is an aesthetically pleasing lesbo love den. In order to get the most out of your setting you will want to pay attention to a few fundamentals.

light up my life

Nothing screams gynecologist's office like a glaring overhead light. If that's what you are working with, invest in a few table lamps, a dimmer switch, or some candles—preferably all three. There's nothing more mood-killing than bright, unflattering light. Lamps give a softer, more flattering light, and candles make everyone look dreamy. Be careful with candles though. I can not tell you how many times I've fallen asleep after sex and woken up to wax all over my nightstand and floor. It's a good thing I've never burned down the house.

music

Music puts you in the mood. It adds instant romance to your sexcapades, and also drowns out sex noises so your roommates don't get grossed out. Make some sex playlists for your iTunes or iPod so that when you are ready to go, you just need to turn the music on. For years I'd just put my iTunes on shuffle and get lulled into a false sense of security by a block of Barry White only to be rudely ripped from my orgasmic lull by the Toreador song from *Carmen*. Don't let this happen to you.

your bed

What's your bed like? Is it comfortable? Is it good for sex? Is it big enough? Take stock of your bed situation and make sure you are offering your potential tricks a nice place to relax and enjoy themselves. Change the sheets before your date in case you get lucky. Keep clean towels handy in case your booty call is a squirter.

your nightstand drawer

This is where all the important, easy-to-reach items get stashed. It's too small for your sex-toy arsenal, but you'll definitely want to keep a few important sundries handy. A small vibrator, latex gloves, condoms, dental dams, baby wipes for quick clean up, and a couple of small toys like a butt plug and perhaps some restraints can get you through an entire night. Or whatever.

your kitchen

Make sure you have coffee, tea, and accouterments on hand for the morning. It's romantic to lie around in bed and discuss last night's sexcapades.

getting busy

DYKES ARE CREATIVE in bed. Take a look at any lesbian erotica anthology and it will contain scenes of clit play, oral sex, handballing, cocksucking, BDSM, dildos, anal sex, fisting, dirty talk, mommy/boy and daddy/girl fantasies, fetishes, spanking, piercing, frottage, tribading, nipple play—the list could go on and on. There's no ultimate act of lesbian sex. Chicks who are fucking chicks are doing it all sorts of ways, swinging from the chandeliers, bent over the kitchen counter, jammed into the front seat of a Chevy, and occasionally lounging in a comfy bed.

So there are a million fun things to do in bed, and where you start depends on what you're into. It also depends on what kind of queer you are and what kind of queer you're fucking.

are you a top or a bottom?

You can be both or either or a switch, you can change your mind halfway through sex. You can top from the bottom and bottom from the top. Or maybe you're thinking, N/A. Top and bottom roles are something that queer women play with and occasionally take very seriously. Have sex with enough queers and you'll probably run into someone who identifies as a stone top, meaning that they fuck but don't get fucked. Or a total bottom which is someone who only receives but doesn't give—or only catches but doesn't pitch, as some like to say.

Sometimes people who don't understand top and bottom roles will criticize them, claiming that these roles are limiting. But that attitude stems from ignorance. It's perfectly OK to be turned on by certain things and not by others. Claiming that everyone should like both getting and giving in bed is no less obnoxious than claiming everyone should like being anally fisted, and for most of us, that's just not how we get down.

topping

Topping can mean a lot of things. Sometimes the top is simply the sexual aggressor. The top is the person who runs the show, but that doesn't necessarily mean that she doesn't get off. Sometimes a top is "stone," meaning she doesn't get touched, she does you and either gets off while she's doing you or on her own time. If you are with a top, you'll probably find that she wants to call the shots and decide who does what to whom. Often a top will want to do you first, and then allow you to get her off in a way that she enjoys. Sometimes a top will get off while she is getting you off, maybe from indirect stimulation to her clit while fucking you with a dildo. The very act of fucking someone and watching them come can make some tops come.

bottoming

The bottom is primarily the receptive partner in sex, though it can mean anything you want it to mean. The bottom can be the one who gets ordered around and performs. The bottom can have her face in the pillow all night. The bottom usually does what the top says. But that doesn't mean bottoms don't set limits and boundaries. There is no hard and fast rule about being a bottom. But if you hook up with someone who tells you she is a bottom, you can assume that she will take a passive role in sex.

how to figure out if you are a top or a bottom

Where does your mind go when you are jerking off? Do you imagine yourself ravaging someone and forcing him or her to submit to your desire? Are you more interested in the thought of penetrating someone than you are in being penetrated? Do you like to hear your lover beg? Are you excited by the prospect of giving your lover orgasms or denying her orgasms if that's how you want to play? Would you feel awkward being on the receiving end of a dildo?

If you answered positively to most of the above questions you are likely a top.

Do you like the idea of being ravished by your lover? Do you want to be taken and forced to submit to someone's will? Are you a pig for sensation, constantly wanting to be filled more or fucked harder? Do you like to be on the receiving end of a strap-on?

If you answered yes to most of these questions you are probably a bottom.

But keep in mind that you can be a bottom on Thursday and a Top on Friday. Or a top with one partner and a bottom with another. Sometimes couples switch off top and bottom roles, or sometimes one person tops and then the other person tops all in the same night.

cruising and flagging

CRUISING MEANS ACTIVELY trolling for sex. It doesn't matter where you are—in a park, bar, club, grocery store, or sex party. Cruising is the art of making suggestive eye contact, starting up a brief conversation, and heading off for a no-strings romp. One thing that makes cruising extra fun is flagging. Flagging is the art of indicating your sexual proclivities with differently colored hankies worn in your back pocket. In other words, it's cruising with accessories!

flagging

In flagging, a hanky worn on the right indicates you are a bottom, and the activity you are cruising for is one that you'd like to have done to you. If your hanky is on your left, you are a top and you'd like to do that particular activity to someone else.

Usually hankies are worn in back pockets, but I've seen femmes get creative and tie them to handbags or tuck them into boots.

The basic colors you'll see on dykes are listed below, though the complete hanky code is mind-bogglingly long and covers nearly every sexual activity you could possibly imagine. Do a Google search for "hanky code" if you are curious.

Light Blue	Cocksucking
Gray	Bondage
Black	Heavy SM
Red	Fisting
Hunter Green	Daddy Play
Mint Green	Mommy Play
Dark Blue	Fucking
Fuchsia	Spanking
Light Pink	Dildos
Dark Pink	Nipple Play
Yellow	Watersports
Olive	Military Scenes
Beige	Rimming
Purple	Piercing
Orange	Anything goes

It's very common to see chicks flagging at leather events, pride events, and sex parties. But more and more it's seen at the bar and other plain old regular places.

don't forget the foreplay

FOREPLAY IS EVERYTHING that leads up to actually getting naked and getting off. Foreplay can be extended bouts of kissing and making out. It can be dirty talk or exchanged fantasies. It can be smutty text messages or e-mails sent during the work day. But whatever form it takes, foreplay is how you prime the pump for what's to come. Foreplay makes sex hotter and better and increases your chances of getting off and getting your partner off.

tips for getting her in the mood

1. Kiss her softly for a long time. Wait until she starts getting frustrated before you kiss her harder.
2. Pull her hair while you kiss her, or put your hands on her face, throat, or the back of her head while you kiss.
3. Take one item of clothing off very slowly and leave the rest on
4. Talk to her. Tell her what you are going to do to her when you finally get her in the bedroom.
5. Run your fingers lightly over her chest and face.
6. Place soft kisses on her neck and shoulders.
7. Lightly touch her nipples with the palm of your hand. If she doesn't want her breasts touched, stroke her back or shoulders instead.
8. Tease your lover by focusing on different body parts for a very long time. Focus all of your attention on her breasts, or her neck, or her lips.

Enthusiastic, strong kissing with lots of tongue and lip play can be very exciting. It makes your lover feel as if she is being devoured. Spend time sucking, licking, nibbling, and stroking parts of her body from the face down. Pay attention to the moans and giggles and comments your lover makes as a way to get acquainted with her turn-ons and turn-offs. Pay close attention in order to glean what her erogenous zones are and what parts are off-limits. Explore her body very thoroughly. This gives you the opportunity to discover what your partner's sexual response is like. Long, hot make-out sessions that don't end in sex are the best way to get someone really interested. Go ahead and get her worked up, and then make her wait for the final treat.

the butch body

Is your lover male-identified? She or he may identify as trans, or maybe he identifies as male gendered in a female body. Many female-bodied dykes are male-identified, or prefer to be seen as male during sex. Regardless of how he describes his gender, he probably wants his female parts approached in certain ways.

some tips for sex with boys of the female variety

Don't be afraid to ask questions. Gender and sex can be sensitive topics, but they don't have to be skirted around. It's OK to say to someone, "How do you like to be touched?"

Some boys prefer to think of their clits as cocks. Refer to it as a "cock" during sex, and refer to oral sex as a "blowjob." Even if your lover isn't strapping at the time, refer to his genitals as a "cock" or "dick."

Does he have breasts? If your lover has breasts he may keep them covered during sex. Don't push him to take off his shirt if he isn't comfortable. If your boyfriend has tits and likes them touched but doesn't want to feel feminine, you can refer to his tits as his "chest" or his "pecs." Remind your boy that gay men love having their nipples played with, and that enjoying nipple stimulation isn't a girly thing.

Don't push for things that your lover doesn't want. This will only cause resentment to build. Let him know that you love his body and see him as masculine regardless of whether he's binding and packing or not. But if he wants to remain clothed during sex, respect his boundaries.

Find other erogenous zones to play with on your boy's body. He may not want his chest caressed, but perhaps his back or shoulders are very sensitive. Pay attention to his responses as you kiss and touch him. Figure out where all the sensitive parts are.

Some boys like to get fucked but don't want to see their cunts as girl parts. Find other things to call it besides "pussy." Try "hole" or another nongendered word.

Never, ever make a butch or boy feel ashamed of his body. Don't draw attention to his tits or cunt if he doesn't want you to.

The ass is an equal-opportunity hole. When I'm with someone masculine-identified, I go for the ass before I go for the cunt. Everyone has an ass—it's not a girly part. Anal sex is hot and faggy. And for a lot of masculine-gendered dykes sex that is reminiscent of gay boy sex is very exciting.

If your butch or boy partner likes penetration, you may want to try out the Feeldoe. It's a silicone double dildo designed by a dyke, and it's definitely the best thing on the market. One end is a thick plug that fits snugly in your puss, and the other end is a cock. Most of the boys I know claim it makes them come like crazy. There is also a version of it made in acrylic called the Transfer. The acrylic version is hard and inflexible and provides the wearer with tons of G-spot stimulation while he or she fucks you.

How does he like to get off? Lots of butches and transguys can come from indirect stimulation, like rubbing against the base of a dildo during sex. Try pressing the base of the dildo against his cunt while you suck his cock.

If he prefers to get you off and then gets himself off on his own time, don't stress him out about it. If it makes sex feel unfinished for you, explain that to him and communicate openly about your needs. He may soften once he realizes how important it is to you to give him pleasure.

Remember that masculinity is complicated in our community, and even if you see him as male, he might not be seen that way once he steps outside his queer world. Let your bed be a safe space for your lover. Bed is where you both get to be whatever the hell you want.

Remember all the tips depend on the person—don't forget to ask what your partner prefers.

breast play

Breasts are sensitive, sexually responsive erogenous zones. And playing with her tits is a good way to turn her on. Some women can even orgasm from intense nipple play.

Everyone loves breasts. And we either want ours touched or we want to touch someone else's—and often we want both. Touching her breasts releases a feel-good hormone called *oxytocin* that gets her entire body geared up for play. If she is into it, you can really get a girl juiced up by stroking her tits and playing around with her nipples.

If your lover girl is more of a boy, play with his tits like you would a gay man's nipples. Pull and pinch the nipples, roll them between your fingers, grip his tits firmly or stroke his chest as if it were flat.

ways to get off on her tits

Cup them in your hands, feel their weight and size.
Wet your fingertips and rub her nipples or blow on them.
Push them together and bury your face between them.
Pull hard on her nipples or pinch them firmly.
Suck her nipples and bite them softly.
Talk dirty to her about her tits, tell her how hot they are.
Play with nipple clamps, clothespins, and other pinchy objects.

show off

Show off your tits for your lover by wearing cleavage-baring outfits or tight, thin T-shirts, if that's what you're into. I've watched entire tables of butches and trannyboys transfixed by a femme baring cleavage. If you want to teach your lover how to touch your tits, start by putting on a little show for her. Run your hands over your breasts and pull and pinch your nipples the way you like to have them touched. Ask her if she likes your body, if she likes your breasts. Display your tits to her as if they are a gift and then ask her to touch them while you touch them. Place your hands on her hands and direct her. Get into a rhythm and move her hands and fingers around with your own so she's stroking you while being guided by your touch.

talk about tits

Talk to your partner about her breasts. Don't just assume that she does or doesn't like them touched. How we feel about our tits has very little to do with gender identity. Just as many feminine women feel ambivalent about their tits as masculine dykes get off on having them played with.

communicate with your lover about sex

TALKING ABOUT SEX and fantasies when you are in a nonsexual setting can be thrilling. Bring up last night's sex while having coffee with your lover in the morning. Mention what parts of the sex were especially exciting and praise her on her mad bedroom skills. You lover will make a mental note of your feedback and the praise you gave her and head in that direction the next time the two of you are in bed.

Bring up sex on a regular basis. Make sex talk a part of your communication. Don't wait until there's a problem—talk about sex as if it's simply a part of your day. Get comfortable with a sexual vocabulary. Talking about sex won't ruin the spontaneity or kill the mystery by making it seem banal. Instead it will infuse all of your activities with a sexual charge. Learn to treat sex as something special and wonderful but also normal and shame-free.

Improve your sexual communication skills

While on a date with a lady you're sexually involved with, bring up something you'd like to do later that night. You'll want to begin by first steering the conversation toward sex.

Compliment your date on her outfit or appearance. Tell her that her new short haircut makes her look really hot or that the dress she's wearing is sexy. Remind her that you find her really attractive and sexually exciting and then find a way to insinuate one of your desires into the conversation. You have to be subtle so she gets a hint of what you are saying but is left wondering whether you are trying to tell her something. You can tell her you had a dream she was holding you down while you were fucking, or maybe tell her it turns you on to think about how hot her body looks when she's on all fours. Whatever your fantasy is, talk about it in a subtle sexy way so the suggestion of sex is in her head for the rest of the evening.

practice talking in bed

One of the easiest ways to communicate about sex is to learn to talk about it while you are actually having it. I don't mean you should start barking out instructions while she's between your legs munching away, but a few whispered requests or firm commands can really start the activity in a direction you are fantasizing about. I'm talking about talking dirty, folks. Talking dirty gets you laid.

Tell your lover how to touch you while you are in bed with her. Learn to say explicit things. Teaching yourself to become comfortable with dirty words and sex talk is one of the best gifts you can give yourself and your sex partners in terms of improving your sex life.

Now, don't start giving someone a lecture about Foucault's theories of sexuality while you are finger-banging her. What I'm talking about is a few well-placed "I like the way you are touching me"s or "Please do that harder"s. Talking dirty can be as simple as saying "I want you." Or it can be a really smutty pornographic monologue. Sometimes people simply mutter sex words while they are getting it on—a string of obscenities can be really hot. Or dirty talk can take the form of a set of strict instructions. I had a lover who had really mastered this skill. She'd wait till we were at a crucial point in our sexcapade and whisper nastily in my ear that I should pull down my panties, turn around, and stick my ass in the air and my face in the pillow. And you'd better bet I did what she told me. Who would resist instructions like that?

I love to talk dirty. It's practically an instant knicker-wetter. I've been totally uninterested in someone sexually and then had them suddenly bust out with some dirty, smutty suggestion about how she or he wants his cock sucked and the next thing you know cartoon hearts are popping out of my eyes. And name-calling? Don't even get me started on how hot that is. Try calling your special lady friend by some nasty names or maybe some sweet ones. She can be your "baby," your "slut," your "nasty whore," your "beautiful goddess." If she's more of a boy, she can be your "stud," your "daddy," your "bad little boy," your "dog." The possibilities are endless.

Learning some basic sexual communication skills can really take your sex life to a new level. When you tell a partner what you want, you improve the sex for both of you. She shouldn't have to guess how you want to be fucked any more than you should be lying in bed frustrated wishing she'd flip you over and do you in the ass.

gaining a sexy vocabulary

Try talking dirty with a new lover. If the words feel weird in your mouth, start out by reading erotica out loud in bed until you are comfortable with a dirty vocabulary.

Once the words feel good to you, try describing what she's doing to you as she's doing it. Or ask her what she wants in very explicit terms. And keep asking until she tells you. Don't let her get away with a simple shrug or "I don't know, I like everything." She doesn't mean that. She knows exactly what she wants, she's just too shy to tell you. Keep at it until you get her to talk to you. This game in itself can be exciting. You'll feel a sense of power by having command of the sex talk, and she'll feel excited that you are encouraging her to voice her desires.

other forms of sex communication

E-mail is a great seduction tool. People check their e-mails all day at work, and a well-written spicy e-mail can send someone's thoughts reeling toward messed-up sheets and wet panties. But beware the spam filter! You never know if her company is monitoring her work e-mail or not. Keep it to gmail, ladies, and you can't go wrong.

If you feel shy about asking for something in bed, try asking for it in e-mail. I've received e-mails from lovers hinting around about being tied up, spanked, or played with in a certain way and gone all Jell-O-like with the anticipation of our next date. Try writing your lover a romantic sexy e-mail. Use dirty words if you feel comfortable doing that. If not, hint around about sex without actually saying it out right. Sentences like "I can't wait to see you again" and "I can't stop thinking about your hands on my body" are extremely sexy without being explicit. But if you feel comfortable with pornographic language, then by all means full speed ahead. I once received an e-mail from my girlfriend that was so profoundly dirty that I had an orgasm while reading it. I kid you not. Right there at my desk. I made the mistake of telling that story to one of my coworkers and he refused to ever e-mail me again.

text messaging

Everyone agrees sex texts rule. Sex texting is a very popular seduction tool. By nature a sex text has to be succinct, which forces you to get right to the point. The direct nature of a sex text increases the sexual urgency and overall hotness of the situation.

Sex texts are clandestine. They are like little sexual reconnaissance missions. Want to turn your lady friend on while she's having a girl's night out? Send her a sex text. And the morning-after text message is a hot way of checking in and telling someone what a nice time you had the night before. It's possible to have an entire sexual encounter over text messaging. And if you are thinking that text messaging is a poor substitute for talking to each other, or the medium is distancing, *au contraire, ma cherie*. Text messaging is queer and dirty. Text messages can be shocking, unexpected, and totally unadorned. You can't write a lot of purple prose in a text message. There's not a lot of room to get fancy in 200 characters or less. A good sex text message gets right to the point.

the dirtiest text messages

I took a sample poll of about fifty queer women from Brooklyn, San Francisco, Boston, and Chicago about the hottest text messages they'd ever received. Perhaps their answers will inspire you.

"I can't stop thinking about last night."
"My panties are wet from thinking about you."
"I want to feel your wet pussy on my fingers."
"I can't stop thinking about my cock in your ass."
"Your face is so beautiful, I loved watching you come."
"My cunt is sore from your fist."
"I love kissing you."
"You are amazing in bed."
"Your body is perfect. I want to fuck your brains out."
"I can't stop jerking off thinking about you."
"I've been replaying last night over and over."

"I want your mouth on my cunt."

"I loved it when you pulled my hair last night."

"Please come over and fuck me."

"You have a great ass."

"Your legs are beautiful."

"I loved feeling your arms around me this morning."

"Your kisses are amazing."

"Your pussy is like a drug, I want more."

"I just jerked off on a pair of panties."

"I'm going to fuck your ass till you come."

"You are so pretty I want to kiss you."

"I loved feeling your mouth against my neck."

"Get over here and get in my bed."

"Come over, I need to see you right now."

"I want your cock in my ass."

"I want your face between my legs."

"I love the way you smell."

"I want to throw you down and fuck you silly."

"I love the way your body feels under my hands."

"I want to make you come over and over."

"I love your eyes."

"I like looking at your mouth while you speak."

"Your lips turn me on."

"I like your lips wrapped around my cock."

"You are the most beautiful woman I've ever seen."

periods of celibacy

WE ALL GO through times where we are alone and not having sex. Whether chosen or not, there are periods in every life when we have no lovers in our beds, no messages on our voicemail, no e-mails from suitors in our inbox. It's understandable to feel down on ourselves or lonely during these periods, but it isn't necessary to feel that way. Having a period of celibacy is a good time to recharge your sex-and-dating battery so you are ready for the next onslaught of attention and adoration.

When you're in the middle of a dry spell, your very best tool for dealing with your alone time is a good single friend. Don't make the mistake of hanging out with your coupled friends regardless of how much you love them. Couples are well meaning, but often the intimacy they share can screw up your perception of singleness. Their steadfast support of each other can make you feel as if your life is inadequate without someone there to support you. Or their cutesy coupley banter and roles can turn you off relationships for good! A single friend can be your back-up date to big events where you might possibly meet someone, or can protect you from meeting someone if that's how you want to roll. Your single friend can be there for you when you are lonely and fill a need for affection and companionship that will keep you from falling in bed with the next stud that walks by just because you've been spending one too many nights at home watching LOGO.

A period of celibacy or singleness is no time to shut down. Look at it as a time to celebrate yourself.

things to do when you are having a celibacy break

Go to the gym.

Take yoga (Bikram yoga especially gives you a great ass).

Shop. Throw out all the old clothes that make you feel like a big frump, and start new with clothes that show off your Bikram yoga ass and make you feel like a stud.

Read more.

Teach yourself a new skill.

Learn something fabulous that isn't practical. For instance, when my friend and I had just moved to Brooklyn and were single and lonely, we decided to learn everything there is to know about bourbon. We read up on different types of bourbon, we did taste tests, we bought books on the history of bourbon. Now we're connoisseurs. It's not that practical, but it does impress dates at parties.

Work on yourself. Work on making you the best possible you. Take classes, read, write, start a blog, make a film, write a memoir. It's involving yourself in things that gets you out and puts you in situations where you can meet fabulous people. Get involved with a cause you feel strongly about.

Go to sex parties. And if you live in some unfabulous town where they don't have dyke sex parties, well, girl, travel. Go back to chapter 4 and reread the "Where the Girls Are" section.

Throw an impromptu dinner party. Call up some of the single girls and boys you know, anyone who doesn't know how to cook, and make something easy and filling like spaghetti and meatballs. You'll have a room full of adoring friends and will feel important and needed and cared for.

Think of the space and time you have away from a lover as a period of rest before things get hectic again. Being single means you can do what you want when you want. You can come home late and not have to check in with anyone. You can enjoy a period of sexual sluttiness, pick up girls in bars, and make out in the bathroom. You can do things alone. You can go to the movies *you* want to see, cook what *you* want for dinner. If you don't want to eat dinner, you don't have to. You can get off any way you like and you don't have to ask anyone for anything. You can have casual sex. You can post an ad on Craigslist for an anonymous trick. You can flirt. You can change your mind as many times as you want and no one will complain. You can invite friends over for dinner and movies. You can have your bed to yourself.

how to kill a dry spell

IF YOU ARE celibate but don't want to be, there are several tried and true methods for killing a dry spell. So if you're ready to start seeing people, socializing, and perhaps getting busy, try these suggestions:

Buy new sex toys. This will get you thinking about sex and make you want to try out your new toys. Attraction is all in the head and people who are thinking about sex draw others to them.

Masturbate frequently. All the time. Jerk off. Go ahead and embrace your inner chronic masturbator. Get really kinky with yourself. Do it in front of a mirror, use toys, make yourself come as many times as you can in one session. Then before you go out, jerk off until you are really close to coming and stop. Set yourself free on the world while you are all horny and turned on.

Sex makes you hot. I think you'll find that once you hook up with someone, your self-protective walls will come down a little bit and people will find themselves drawn to you. The minute you start getting action, everyone will want a piece. We're all drawn to the person that's getting laid. We think of them as where the sex is.

jerking off: it's sex with someone you love

If you are masturbating, you are being sexual. And being sexual makes you sexy. When you get yourself off, you are creating a sexuality that exists outside of a partner. This is a concept many of us struggle with—we get caught up in thinking we must be responding to another person's desire in order to be sexual. But why should we feel asexual when we aren't with a partner? We don't question our sexual orientation. We're still queer even if we don't have a girlfriend or boyfriend, and we're still sexual even if we don't have a lover. Masturbation and fantasy are ways to be sexual without the presence of another person.

Jerking off is like taking a vacation alone—it grants you independence. Getting to know your body and figuring out new ways to get off teaches you all sorts of things about your sexual response that you can then teach to a lover. Did you know it was possible to retrain your sexual response? Well, it is.

Try something new next time you are taking a little masturbation break. Don't get frustrated if it doesn't get you off at first. Relax and pay attention to the sensations. Let yourself enjoy what's going on without worrying about when or if you are going to come. Let new feelings wash over you and follow them as they move throughout your body. Does it feel particularly good when you push a dildo against your G spot? Or tug on your labia? What about your nipples? Note the sensations and let yourself experience them. You might just find yourself getting off in ways you didn't think were possible.

CHAPTER 8

sex: taking it to the sheets

SO MUCH FOR the sex theory. Let's move on to the sex practice. We know how to get a girl in bed, and how to have a great sex life with her once she's there. But now I'm going to give you a few specifics to do with a queer lady once you get her in your bed.

what's in your toy chest?

EVERY GOOD DYKE needs a sex-toy collection. Sure, its possible to have great sex without sex toys—it's also possible to put together a great outfit together without accessories. But that doesn't mean you should.

Your toy chest can contain just the basics or it can be an entire rec room full of fun. If you are having casual sex, there are a couple of items you'll want to make sure you have on hand. One of these is a smallish vibrator such as a Pocket Rocket.

Always offer your special friend a vibrator if she has difficulty coming. She may be too shy to ask for one or afraid of offending you. Keep it handy and stocked with fresh batteries so you are always prepared. Other must-haves include safer-sex supplies such as latex gloves and at least two different types of lube— a thicker one for fun activities where you need a little extra cushioning like anal play or vaginal fisting and a thinner, more

watery one for other activities. You'll also want to stock up on
dental dams and condoms.

how to choose sex toys

When putting together a sex-toy collection, consider what types
of stimulation you like, what feels good, how you like to get
off, and what types of things you might want to do with your
partner.

vibrators

Vibrators vibrate. Sometimes we need the steady thrum of
stimulation that a vibrator provides. Vibrators are like tireless
little orgasm soldiers. All they need is fresh batteries and they are
always ready to go. If you require a lot of clit attention, invest in
a good vibrator.

plug-in vibrators

Plug-in vibrators like the Hitachi Magic Wand offer a strong
steady throb and two basic settings (throb and jackhammer).
The Hitachi is widely considered to be the Cadillac of vibrators,
and if you've never had an orgasm, sister, go and invest in one of
these babies. Orgasms await you.

There are several knock-off versions of the Hitachi Magic
Wand that work very well. Some are rechargeable so you don't
have to be tethered to the wall. Some are smaller and lighter,
which is nice since the Hitachi is a major appliance. It's like
having your orgasms powered by an upright kitchen mixer. Just
go to the home-electronics store in the mall and try them all out
till you find one you like. Over your clothes, silly! You don't want
to get carted off by security.

Coil-operated vibes like the Wahl offer a super-intense buzz
and a very focused point of contact. And they are so quiet you
can jerk off while your roommate is home and not have to

worry. They are also strong and long-lasting like the Hitachi but much smaller and easier to maneuver. These things never die. I had one for fifteen years—three times as long as any relationship I've ever been in. I finally threw it out because I was sick of moving it from apartment to apartment. Coil-operated vibes come with lots of attachments and many outside companies make even more attachments that fit them. This type of vibrator, like other plug-ins, usually only offers two speeds, but their steady, strong vibrations are what many women need to have regular orgasms.

battery-operated vibrators

Battery-operated vibrators come in all shapes, sizes, and colors. They are usually less intense than plug-ins and don't last as long. But they are far less expensive and offer many options in terms of size, speed, intensity and shape. Two popular options are the Silver Bullet and the Pocket Rocket. The Bullet is very versatile—you can put it in a condom and pop it in whatever orifice you want while you are going down on someone. And the Rocket is good because it's strong, durable and small enough to use during sex with a partner.

For the most part battery-operated vibrators are louder than plug-ins. This is because the motor and the batteries themselves are rattling around inside a plastic casing. But fear not! Several companies have caught on to the fact that we don't necessarily want the neighbors to know every time we bust out our special plastic friend. A company called Fun Factory makes silicone battery-operated vibrators that are extremely quiet, well designed, and durable. Some are rechargeable so you don't have to worry about batteries. If you want a high-quality battery-operated vibe, check out Fun Factory's toys at your local sex-toy store.

dildos

Oh, dildos! How I love thee. Dildos are like spare boyfriends that just hang out under your bed waiting for you to call them. To some of us, it's just a toy. To others, a dildo is our cock, period. It's not a toy, it's not made of silicone, it's the physical manifestation of the cock that we have psychically 24/7. To others, it's a sex toy we strap on to have fun with, and to others still, it's something that we get fucked with but would never even think of strapping on. Regardless of how you think of your dildo, you know you love it.

Dildos come in all shapes and sizes and are made of all sorts of materials. But take my advice and buy a silicone dildo. The other types of mystery rubber aren't really that much cheaper and mystery rubbers aren't stable—meaning they can leach chemicals called phylates into your bloodstream. You know that plastic smell when you open the package? That's phylates. The smell is caused by something called outgassing—small molecules of the plastic or rubber actually break off and float around in the air. Your pussy and your butt are both mucus membranes, and they allow chemicals a straight shot to your bloodstream. You don't want to put some unstable chemicals in there. Phylates have been linked to breast cancer, cervical cancer, and other yucky illnesses.

OK, that said. If you really like those cyberskin porn-star dicks, and I know a few of you who do, then go ahead and buy one. But always put a condom on it. A condom will protect you from chemicals and from any bacteria that might grow on the porous surface of your willy. Other popular nonsilicone options are jelly cocks. Some dykes like these because they are extra bendy and therefore good for packing. Go ahead and get one if you want, but use a rubber. Every time.

Silicone cocks last forever. Silicone is stable and inert. You can boil them, stick them in the dishwasher, bleach them, and wash them with soap and water. There are several new types of silicone on the market. Both Vixen Creations and Tantus Silicone, the two big players in the silicone toy industry, have created silicone cocks that look and feel like the cyberskin ones. Check them out at your local toy palace.

So what size willy do you want? I can't really tell you what size to buy, but I can offer up a few tips that might help you make a decision. First of all, if you are buying it to use on your partner, you will probably be tempted to buy a gigantor monster dick. Because, of course, everyone wants a big dick, right? Well, she might like that, but chances are she won't really be able to take it. Your eyes are probably much larger than her pussy—and what fun is it to have a monster in your pants that you can't use on anyone? Go for a more moderate size and get a bigger one later if you both agree that's what you want. The same rule applies if you are buying it for yourself. Start small. Especially if you want to use it anally. If you are looking for a dildo for butt play, start really small and move up as you get more relaxed.

nipple thingies

Do you like to have your nipples played with? Then go get yourself a set of nipple clamps. Nipple clamps make you feel all sexy and kinky, and they feel fantastic. Nipple clamps come in all sorts of varieties. There are vibrating ones, weighted ones, ones with teeth, ones that hurt, and ones that don't. Your main goal when buying nipple clamps is to make sure you don't buy some that clamp so tightly you can't bear it. Adjustable ones are a good way to go. And clothespins make a great set of nipple clamps, so you may want to start out playing with clothespins and then move up to something shiny and metallic.

butt toys

Everyone can have fun with their butt. Butt play isn't weird or kinky. It doesn't make you a perv, unless you want to stick a watermelon or a Cocker Spaniel in there. Your butt is an equal-opportunity orifice, so if you aren't friendly with your lady parts, you can still have fun with your butt.

There are lots of fun things to stick in your butt. Butt plugs are a good place to start. If you are buying a butt plug, read the lecture about silicone in the "Dildos" section before shopping. And then if you decide you still want to purchase a nonsilicone butt toy, go ahead—but always use a condom. Actually you should put condoms on your butt toys anyway because it makes clean up much nicer.

If you are new to butt play, start with the smallest plug you can find. If you end up loving it and want something bigger, you can always go get another one. But there's nothing more disappointing than buying a new toy that you can't use.

Anal beads are another fun butt-play option. These are a series of plastic beads attached to a string. You push them in and then pop them out one by one. The cheap plastic ones aren't really washable so using them more than once is likely a no-no. But there are lots of anal bead–like options made of silicone. Some are simply anal beads dipped in silicone, and some are more like a long stick of silicone that has bloops of graduated sizes along the shaft.

Glass, acrylic, and metal

Some of my very favorite insertable toys are made of glass, acrylic, and stainless steel. Toys made of these materials often look like works of art. The benefit to these materials is that they are extremely firm and nonporous so the lube lasts extra long.

Glass, acrylic, and metal toys are often a sizeable financial investment so unless you really fall in love with something, these are probably not going to be the first additions to your toy chest.

Glass toys are made by a variety of companies, and they are all roughly the same. So if you are interested in glass, you'll probably have many options to choose from. The coolest stainless-steel toys are made by a company called Njoy. They have a beautiful selection and the weight and shape of these toys make them powerful G-spot stimulators. The coolest acrylic toys are made by Cox Industries. Check out their wares at www.artislove.com.

And if you like the idea of a double dildo, but haven't found anything that works for you. I highly recommend the Transfer, an acrylic double dildo based on the same design as the Feeldoe. It's a very impressive toy and has many devoted followers.

getting busy

Now that we've covered sex toys, let's get down to business with the sex tips. There are many things to do with a lady in bed, and the following options are just some ideas to get you started.

going down

Aside from being the most basic and expected art of the whole lesbo sex repertoire, oral sex is the single fastest route to orgasm for many women. Many of us need direct clitoral stimulation in order to get off, and oral sex can give your girl what she needs. No two women are alike, and you'll have to experiment to find out what flips her switch. Some girls like it more than others. For some women it's the be-all and end-all of the whole sexual experience—some girls have oral sex exclusively—and some find having their partner down there with their face hidden to be a little alienating. If she likes it and you like it, then by all means go forward and eat pussy.

Here are a few tips and techniques you can try.

Start off slowly. Tease her. Work your way down her body. Don't just dive in.

Use your fingers, touch her, talk to her. Warm her up. Do whatever you normally do to get in the mood. Then commence with the cunnilingus.

Nuzzle your lips against her vulva, then lightly lick her inner labia and move your way up. Then work your tongue between her labia and lick up toward the top of her mons until you feel her erect clit. Hold still and let her feel the build of anticipation. Pay close attention to cues. If she's inching toward your face, you are in good shape.

Try using a wide flat tongue to stimulate her entire vulva. Lick lightly up and down for as long as you like. Move languidly around her entire vulva, letting her feel the pressure of your tongue.

When you think you have her sufficiently warmed up, begin to pay more attention to her clit. Try different tongue positions and shapes. A hard pointed tongue is very useful for making small, tight circles around her clit, while a softer tongue can lick up and down over her clit and hood. Start with one technique and switch to the other after a few minutes. With pussy-eating it's important to build up a rhythm but not to stay in the same rhythm so long that she gets bored. Take little breaks from the clit every few minutes and concentrate on other areas. Her clit is where you want to pay most of your attention. But moving away from it and coming back will build the tension without overstimulating her. If you concentrate on the clit too soon it's possible she'll get worked up but not be able to go the distance. So dance around her clit and all over her vulva until she's at the breaking point.

Most women orgasm in response to direct rhythmic clitoral stimulation. If you've gotten her close, which you should be able to judge by her body language and the sounds she's making, start concentrating all your attentions on her clit.

Find a beat and stick to it. You can switch between just moving your tongue and moving your jaw and head when your tongue begins to tire.

vaginal penetration

Vaginal penetration can be a side dish to oral sex and other clit stimulation, or it can be the main dish. For some, it's our preferred method of orgasm, and for others, it's a once in a while treat. Some women respond to G-spot stimulation, some like the feeling of thrusting, and some want to be filled to the brim with a fist or large dildo. Even if being fucked isn't what gets you off, you might enjoy the feeling you get when someone penetrates you.

There are so many things you can do with a pussy. Most of us find our clits to be the most sensitive part of our anatomy and need stimulation of our clits in addition to penetration in order to get off. But ya never know. Not only is every dyke different but sometimes the same cooch can respond one way on Wednesday afternoon and entirely differently on Friday night. You'll have to ask her to figure out how she likes her clit touched.

finger-fucking

I actually prefer to call this finger-banging because it's funnier, plus "finger-fucking" seems redundant. Of course fingering is fucking, so "finger-fucking" might as well be called "fucking-fucking." But I digress. Finger-fucking is the tried and true way to fuck your girl when you are stuck in an elevator and no one is packing.

Fingers are very sensitive instruments. You can feel every little bit of your partner's coochie with your fingers. You can bend your fingers in all sorts of ways to reach all the most sensitive spots. You can fuck your partner with one or two fingers, or you can slowly add fingers until you have four fingers inside. She may enjoy a thrusting motion, she may simply want to feel filled up, or she might want you to move your fingers around inside her stroking and touching different parts of her pussy.

Stimulate your partner's G spot by curling your fingers toward the front of her vagina. The G spot will be a ridged, spongy, bumpy section on the front wall of her vag. Rub this spot firmly and you may find that it makes your special lady ejaculate as she comes. Penetrating your partner with one hand means that the other hand is free to stimulate her clit or simultaneously penetrate her ass.

when four fingers aren't enough

Fisting is when you penetrate your partner with your entire hand. It's a slow process—you don't just jam your fist into someone. You work up to it, four fingers, then add the thumb, then fold your hand up and gently push it past the vaginal opening. Your hand naturally curls up into a ball as you push it in, thus the term "fisting." Sometimes if you are very lucky, four fingers will turn into five and the next thing you know, oops! Your fist is inside someone. Wow!

Fisting generally takes time and patience and slow, precise movements. It involves trust and willingness. The person being fisted has to want to be fisted. Intense penetration, whether it's anal or vaginal, is mostly about your head. If you really want something and you are very aroused, your body will be open and receptive. If you are afraid or nervous, your muscles will contract and you won't be able to take your partner's hand.

Fisting is a lot easier than you'd think. Your pussy is stretchy—babies come out of it after all. Not only that, but when you are very aroused, your cunt does this amazing thing called tenting. It balloons out and expands, creating lots of room in which to fit a fist. Some people can even take two fists, though that's something you've really got to work up to.

Use a latex glove for fisting unless you and your partner have agreed not to use barriers with each other. Coat your entire hand with copious amounts of water-based lube. Begin by working two fingers into her pussy and slowly work up to four fingers. Rotate and thrust the four fingers at the entrance to her vag to help her open up. Then, when she feels open and ready, tuck your thumb into your palm and fold your hand so that it is as narrow as possible.

Once you've gotten this far you are just about ready for the rest of it. Push your hand into her until the widest part of your hand is at the entrance to her cunt. Rotate your hand a few times as you ease it past the tight ring of muscle at the vaginal opening. Go very slowly and add lube often. Soon your hand will disappear into her pussy. You'll notice as you make your way in that it naturally starts to curl into a fist. Next thing you know you are in your lady up to the wrist. Lucky you.

Once inside keep your movements to a minimum. If she wants you to thrust, she will let you know. But unless you guys are fisting pros, she's probably pretty overwhelmed by the feeling of a whole hand in there. So take it slowly.

It's easiest to remove your fist by letting her force it out as she comes. But this might not always happen. So be prepared to ease it out when she has had enough. Don't pull out suddenly— it can be painful. Instead work your way out of her vag as slowly as you went in. Talk to her during the entire process. You should be checking in with her about how everything feels. Let her guide you.

You can combine fisting with all sorts of other forms of stimulation like vibrators or fingers on her clit. Or she may find being fucked like this so intense that she wants nothing more than to ride the wave of sensation you are giving her. Fisting is very intense. Sometimes being fisted can cause your partner to ride on the edge of orgasm for a very long time because it is such an overwhelming sensation. If this is the case she may need a vibrator or some other type of direct clit stimulation to get over the edge.

strap-on sex

Strap-on sex means strapping on a dildo in order to fuck your partner. There are lots of harnesses designed for this—head to any sex toy store and you'll find an array of sizes and colors. My personal favorite is the Spare Parts harness. It's designed by a dyke and it's the sexiest, most secure, and most practical harness I've ever seen.

Wearing a strap-on takes a little practice. It's not the most natural feeling in the world for most of us. And even if we find wearing a dildo to be a righteous turn-on, we still need some time to adjust to having a schlong hanging down between our legs. Try strapping it on over your clothes and wearing it around the house. Do the dishes, vacuum, watch TV. Just get used to sporting a dick.

Fucking your partner with a strap-on takes a little practice, but it can be a very rewarding experience for both of you. If you are really into the idea of having a cock and you identify with it as an extension of your body, then thrusting inside your partner might be enough to get you off.

The receptive partner may require some clitoral stimulation in order to have an orgasm. If she's on her hands and knees and you are fucking her from behind, she can reach between her legs and stroke her clit. She can also use a vibrator in this position.

Some harnesses come with a small sewn-in pouch that holds a bullet vibrator. This can give some extra clit attention to the wearer. Or the wearer can reach behind the base of her dildo and stroke her clit while she is thrusting inside you.

packing

"Packing" is when you wear a dildo under your clothes. You can "pack hard" by sporting a dick you can fuck with, or "pack soft," by wearing either a cyberskin "packy" or just some rolled-up socks. The bulge is intended to make you feel sexy and draw

tried and true positions

KNEELING BETWEEN HER LEGS: you are between her legs and she's on her back or stomach.

DOGGY-STYLE: she's on her hands and knees and you are kneeling behind her.

MISSIONARY POSITION: she's lying on her back and you are lying on top of her.

GIRL ON TOP: you are on your back and she is straddling you.

SIDE BY SIDE: You are both on your side and the receptive person has one leg thrown over the other person's waist.

BENT OVER: the receptive person is bent over something like a couch, bed or table. The other person is standing behind her.

everyone's eyes to your crotch.

Packing a cock is exciting. It indicates a readiness for sex, and that gets chickies turned on. Also, when you are packing, you are prepared for a quickie. Some dykes like to pack because they find the process of strapping on their cocks before sex to be too laborious and kind of a mood dampener. They'd rather be able to drop trou and whip it out.

Packing requires a dick flexible enough to bend. Cyberskin and jelly cocks are good for this, though be sure to use condoms since those materials contain chemicals you don't want in your cooch.

Strap on your monster and either tuck it into a jock strap or wear an extra set of briefs to help batten it down. You can wear it sticking up or pushed into the crook between your crotch and thigh. Both look sexy beneath a pair of jeans—or a skirt if you're kinky.

Try wearing your dick out on the town and watch ladies' eyes stray to your crotch. Wear it to a sex party and be as prepared as a Boy Scout. Or just wear it over to your lady friend's house and bone her brains out all night.

how to suck cock

I'm talking about strap-on cock, of course. If you've never considered engaging in silicone cocksucking, you are in for a treat. Cocksucking gives the wearer an incredible show, and the cocksucker gets not only to feel like the hottest thing in the world but to enjoy having something in her mouth. Lots of women can get off this way, both from penetrating someone's mouth or having their mouth penetrated. It just takes a little retraining.

As the suckee, think psychic cock. It's not just a cock. It's an outward manifestation of your hard-on. Think about that dick between your legs as your dick. Concentrate on how it feels to have your cock in someone's mouth.

As the sucker, put on a good show. Roll your tongue around the head of the cock, licking and swirling the tip so that your partner can enjoy watching your mouth move around his or her dick. Try taking as much of it into your mouth as possible. If it's too long, wrap your hand around the base of the dildo to keep yourself from accidentally gagging. As you wrap your hand around the base, push the cock against her clit to give her extra stimulation. Alternate sucking on the head with taking it into your mouth with one long stroke. Look up at her as you do this.

How are you positioned? Being on your knees in front of your partner can be visually thrilling for both of you. If you are getting blown, try putting your hand on your partner's head or grabbing her by the hair and guiding her mouth. Bottomy gals will literally eat this up.

Sometimes the idea of having your dick in someone's mouth

is enough to get you off. Visualize what it would be like to come this way. If you concentrate on it, you can retrain yourself to get off like this.

how to deal with problem orgasmer

Is she a tough nut to crack? Don't make her feel guilty or weird about it. Lots of us have trouble coming. Orgasms are all in the head. While the orgasm itself is a physiological response, the way you arrive at it is all about your brain. And if she feels insecure, nervous, unloved, or unwanted in some way, she might have trouble coming.

Talk to her about her orgasms. Find out how she comes when she is alone. Does she use her hand? What about a vibrator? Offer her a vibe if she usually uses one to get herself off. Encourage her to talk about her fantasies. It's possible that she needs something she's too shy to talk about. Watch porn together and pay attention to her sexual responses. You might just learn a thing or two about the person you are bedding.

do you want to come more easily?

One of the first things you can do to make yourself orgasm more easily is to realize that the person who is fucking you wants to be there. And that getting you off is a huge source of pleasure for them. And if you have doubts about whether the person wants to have sex with you, you probably shouldn't be having sex with them.

If you are a slow come, try switching to a new activity. If you are having oral sex, ask your partner to use her hand. If you are fucking, switch to oral sex. Change it up. Sometimes a new set of nerves will respond more quickly than ones that have been receiving pleasure for a while.

Try visualizing what's happening to you while it's being done. Pay close attention to the sensations. Make sure that you are extremely turned on before you start thinking about having an orgasm. Don't just go for the gold. Spend a long time working up to it.

Try not to hold your breath. In fact, take deep breaths and picture the oxygen going into your pelvic area. You want your body to feel engorged and full of blood. Clenching your muscles or holding your breath stops blood flow to the pelvic region.

Use your vibrator during sex. Or stimulate yourself with your fingers while your partner is fucking you. Fantasize. Let your mind wander to your nastiest, most taboo fantasies. They might help push you over the edge. You can also try visualizing yourself coming—sometimes this helps us connect to the sensations that create orgasm.

Don't limit yourself to the things I've described in this chapter. These are just a few suggestions to get you going for those nights when your date goes really well. I haven't even touched on BDSM, sensation play, anal sex, rough sex, vanilla sex, role play, age play, games, public sex, fantasies, and so much else. Our bodies and brains are amazing and the way dykes fuck and get off varies widely.

Want to be a better lover? Read books and attend workshops. Talk about sex with your lovers. Learn to understand what they want and what you want. Pay attention to the clues she gives you. Don't be afraid to experiment and don't be afraid of intimacy. Sex is wonderful and we all deserve to have as much of it as we want.

part three

post-dating survival

CHAPTER 9

dyke drama

DYKE DRAMA. IT'S the bane of dating girls. It's what makes our relationships exciting, and it's what occasionally makes them a living hell. You've probably heard about it. Now I'm going to tell you what it is and what causes it.

The number one cause of dyke drama is that girls can't keep it in their pants. Anytime you have a large group of dykes together, they are all probably about one degree of separation from one another. There are only so many of us, and eventually everyone you know will have slept with everyone else you know. And then everyone is in everyone else's sexual tree. In fact, if you are reading this book, you are probably in my sexual tree. Dykes just can't seem to remain "just friends."

processing

THE FIRST THING you are going to have to learn about dyke drama is how to process. Processing is the way dykes communicate. No matter what your actual gender or sexual orientation is—you can be a straight girl having a fling or a transman dating a high femme—but if you are dating a girl and you aren't actually a straight man, you're going to have to process.

Everything is just a little more emotionally charged between two girls. Sex, money, jealousy, possessiveness, need, want, security, insecurity, stability, safety, all these things are closer to the surface. Part of it is due to the fact that we're having relationships that aren't totally welcome everywhere. Sure, dykes are accepted more and more and queerness is less shocking to mainstream society now than in the past. But it's still not OK. Not really. And the ramifications of this are far-reaching. The lack of safety we feel as marginalized members of society can leach over into our relationships and we begin to hold our partners accountable for things that are beyond their control. Simply existing in a society that doesn't fully embrace lesbian relationships can mean a low level of continuous anxiety for many queer women. It's like constantly being on orange alert. And often it surfaces as controlling, needy, demanding, or insecure behavior.

Also, women talk about things. We communicate differently from most men. Of course, this doesn't hold true for all women, and I'm not trying to be reductive. But many of us were raised to talk about our feelings in ways that most men were not. We assuage our anxiety by communicating about what's going on in our lives. We talk to our partners, to our friends, to our families. But sometimes the processing itself is the problem. The whole act of talking about an issue can eclipse the issue itself. We get so caught up in the anxiety-reducing effects of talking through a problem that we don't want to stop. And eventually we've created a whole slew of new problems just so we can go through the process of talking about them.

If you find yourself in a situation where you are constantly processing with your date or your girlfriend about every little thing, ask yourself if the talking is helping or hurting. Working through problems is healthy, but getting caught up in things and missing out on events you were scheduled to attend or constantly having to make excuses for your partner are signs of problems. Sometimes we use processing and our need to talk about issues as a way of emotionally blackmailing someone into giving us attention in an unhealthy way. It's OK to take a break. Give yourself enough time and space away from what you perceive as problems to gain clarity and then go back to talking.

the lesbophone

The lesbophone is the way information travels in the lesbian community. One lesbian talks to another lesbian, and then that lesbian talks to her vet, and then the vet tells her girlfriend, and then the girlfriend posts it on her Livejournal, and then another lesbian reads the entry and tells the lesbian who works at the sex-toy shop in the town you live in, and the next thing you know the information has been efficiently disseminated.

Through the magic of the lesbophone, your ex-girlfriend will find out the minute you go on a date—even if she lives across the country. You will know everything she does and she will know everything you do. Everyone will know when you break up; everyone will know when you get back together. You will have no privacy.

The lesbophone is handy when you need information about someone else, for example when you need to know if the babe who answered your Craigslist ad is really what she seems to be. Ask around: Someone will know someone who dated her in high school or who is best friends with her ex. The lesbophone is slightly less useful when you want to keep your personal life to yourself.

myspace and friendster drama

Myspace and Friendster were invented so dykes could stalk each other from the comfort of their own beds. Everyone is on Myspace and Friendster. If your parents are single, they're probably on Myspace and Friendster. Or Tribe or Facebook or any of the other social-networking sites. These sites have become the new dyke bars. And they are a lot of fun if you use them for good and not for evil.

The problem with everyone being on the various social networking sites is that we've lost any shred of privacy we had, which wasn't much since lesbian communities are small and we all talk to each other on the lesbophone.

myspace or yours?

Blogging is another insidious feature of the social-networking sites. Myspace started the trend, and Friendster rapidly followed suit. Want to know what your girlfriend is doing on the nights you aren't together? Read her friends' blogs. "It's not like Karen is cheating on me or anything like that," says my best friend, Amy, of her girlfriend. "It's just that when I read her friends' blogs, I see all these references to the crazy, drunken nights she has when I'm not around. I wish I didn't know about how so-and-so thinks she's really hot. Every day I tell myself I won't search her Myspace page for references to things I don't need to know about. I'm too embarrassed to complain to her about it. I just wish it wasn't there so I wouldn't feel so compelled to look!"

Social sites succeed based on the principle that you'll get along with your friend's friends and offer you a good excuse to hang out: "Hey, you know Diana, and I know Diana: Let's have coffee."

But in the world of lesbians, they are also a gateway drug for recycling ex-girlfriends. I try not to worry about the expanding branches of my sexual tree, but things went too far the day my ex-girlfriend began leaving Myspace comments for my girlfriend's ex-girlfriend. We're talking dyke drama of such epic proportions it deserves its own *L Word* episode.

And when the respective exes were spotted at a crowded dyke bar, making out like they were underwater and could only get oxygen from each other's faces, I knew about it the next day. Just as you'd guess, that story made Myspace faster than Katie Holmes's cold sore made Defamer.

really, we're just friendsters

Social networking sites like Friendster.com and Myspace.com may have given us a new way to hookup and breakup but Friendster's recent improvements—blogs, slideshows of friends' photos, and a homepage that tracks practically every key stroke of everyone in your friend network—have also made it a perfect tool for stalking your crush and keeping tabs on your ex.

"I was crushed out on some girl all summer long but too afraid to make a move. So instead I just checked her profile constantly looking for some excuse to start up a conversation. Cruising her online was like an addiction," says Barb, one of my many Friendsters. "I couldn't stop looking at her."

Friendster-stalking is so compelling that my ex-girlfriend deleted her account when we broke up because, as she confessed, she couldn't keep herself from looking at my profile ten times a day. I, of course, knew the exact moment it happened because I'd been hitting refresh on her page every five minutes.

It's the update notifications that really suck you in. Every time anyone in your network changes their status from "single" to "in a relationship" you get an e-mail telling you to check out their updated profile. My friend Mary called me the other night freaking out because a girl she'd gone on a few dates with changed her profile status from "single" to "it's complicated."

"Is that some kind of reference to me?" she wailed. "Or do you think she's reconciling with her ex?"

"Why don't you ask her?" I suggested.

"I can't do that," screeched Mary. "She'll know I've been stalking her Friendster profile!"

"I told my therapist I was addicted to Friendster, and she said tons of her clients have confessed the same thing," explains Kelly, a woman I dated about six months ago.

Kelly has been flirting with our mutual friend Angie, which I know because I've been reading the testimonials they keep leaving for each other, growing increasingly cranky with each new in-joke or cutesy reference to time spent together.

The testimonials are right out there in the open for everyone to see, so in theory I shouldn't feel guilty for reading them, but I can't shake the sensation that I'm spying on a private transaction. A few days ago Angie posted a picture of a dinner party at her house, and there was *my* Kelly sitting at the table swilling wine. I'd sure love to know why I wasn't invited, but that would, of course, require me to confess I'd been checking out her profile, wouldn't it?

we're related

Have you ever noticed that all lesbians seem to know each other in some way? I mean, unless you are completely new to dating girls, and you are dating girls who are completely new to dating girls, you'll probably run into this. And even if you are totally new to lesbian land, it's just a matter of time before you date someone who has dated someone you know. So be prepared.

talk to your friends

The best way to deal with possibly dating someone who one of your friends has been involved with is to set boundaries before it ever happens. And if the situation comes up, communicate as openly and honestly as the situation allows. If a friend says an ex is off-limits but you really want to date that person, you need to evaluate how much that friendship means. Is it worth losing a friend who has maybe been in your life for years over a girl who may not be more than a fling? Only you can answer that.

polyamory

Maybe you've heard about polyamory? Literally it means "loving many." It's the act of dating multiple people, having relationships with multiple people, or having one significant or "primary" partner but having other lovers as well. If you are seriously interested in polyamory, there are several books on the subject that can help you in your quest to spread the love around. Start with *The Ethical Slut* by Catherine Liszt and Dossie Easton and *Redefining Our Relationships: A Guideline for Responsible Open Relationships* by Wendy-O Matik.

There's a fine line between successful poly and sleeping around. If you aren't serious about polyamory, don't try it. When done poorly, poly is a good way to add maximum drama to any relationship. And casually fooling around with lots of women is a good way to annoy everyone at once.

If you are dating someone who says she is poly, ask what that means to them. Set clear boundaries and rules. Be clear about your needs and expectations. Will both of you be seeing other people? Will you have specific nights that you see each other? Will you disclose information about your other dates and lovers? These things need to be discussed between the two of you.

is poly dead?

Last week there was a "Missed Connection" ad posted on Craigslist clearly meant for someone I was seeing. Something about "you were the hott butch (sic) and

I was the femme in the white tank top, we shared a smoke." It goes on to suggest that they might run into each other again, and it lists a few places that my special lady friend frequents, which gave it a nice stalkerish touch. There's no mention of passionate snogging outside the club, which is probably why my date didn't mention this friendly little tête-à-tête. And regardless, there's really no reason for me to get my panties in a bunch. Extracurricular activity is totally sanctioned within the tenets of our relationship. We are, as they say, a polyamorous couple. Sorta, kinda.

"I'm only interested in dating other people because you said I should," explained my rather put-upon lover, Gloria. "We have enough trouble just dealing with all of our ex-girlfriends, I can't imagine adding another current one," she added as she rolled her eyes.

It's not that I actually want to have multiple partners, it's that I really hate rules. If I see a rule, I want to break it. And if you forbid me to sleep with someone, that person becomes irresistible. And the more I think about it in this manner, the more I start to wonder, Is poly just another word for slutty?

"You have no boundaries," I was recently told by my friend Mary. This is coming from a woman who lives in an ongoing triad relationship and runs pansexual sex clubs.

I do have some boundaries; they are just different than other people's. For instance, I think that French kissing, much like "Aloha," is a perfect way to say hello or good-bye. Or as my ex put it, "Making out is just like hugging, but with tongue."

"Can Danielle come home with us and watch us have sex?" I asked my lady one night when we'd just started dating. Danielle is one of my closest friends, and it seemed like a nice way to get her and my lover to be comfortable around each other. It's so much cozier than brunch. "Are you serious?" stammered Gloria, which I assumed meant no.

It used to be that everyone around me agreed making out was good sport. All my friends' relationships were fluid and filled with casual hook-ups. But gradually everyone around me paired up and settled down. No one ever wants to go to the sex club with me these days. They all want to stay home and experiment with new recipes. "I'm too tired to be poly anymore," said Danielle when I asked about her relationship recently.

I just read an article about these trendy high school kids in New York who are into getting together in big groups and rolling around on one another affectionately, like giant pandas. They hook up into little groups of two or three and fool around with no worry about couple loyalty or sexual orientation. "I totally relate to that!" I said as I showed the article to my roommate. "Except those kids are too young to drink and you're in your thirties," she replied.

"Getting it on with everyone is only OK if you are totally single—it doesn't work when you have a partner," says Adian, a former boi toy turned serious boifriend.

"But I thought you wanted to be in an open relationship?" I said to him.

"Not anymore. That was just the first few weeks. I don't want to watch Steven make out with lots of guys. If for no other reason than it's unhygienic."

"Doing it with more than one person is way too hard," says Melissa, one of my oldest friends. Melissa and I fooled around a few times about a million years ago, back in the day when we were both just bi-curi-ous, or "bi now, gay later," as I've heard it called. In fact, we didn't just fool around with each other; we fooled around with each other, each other's friends, and girlfriends. Sometimes all at once. But now she's happily partnered up and living in the suburbs with her girlfriend and their dog and cat. "Just thinking about having an open relationship exhausts me. I'm defi-nitely too old to be polyamorous," she says.

"It does seem like a perfect way to live, you know, everyone just trusts everyone and learns to work on their jealousy and possessive shit," says Jennie, a for-merly poly friend of mine with a graphic-design busi-ness. "But I work so much I don't really have time for it now." And then she adds the final blow, "Maybe what you need is a real job."

breakups happen

THE WORST PART about dating is breaking up. Sometimes breakups are drama-free, and sometimes they are even easy, but rarely are they fun. Even when ending a relationship is a relief, it still causes far-reaching ramifications that are difficult to control.

The best way to handle a breakup is to take some time away for yourself. Even if it's just a few days, having a little alone time can help you regain your independence. When you are ready, start hanging out with friends and try and enjoy yourself without wondering what your former girlfriend is doing.

Don't engage in petty behavior. Don't try and get back at an ex who has spurned you. Don't ask friends to take sides. Even if it feels uncomfortable, know that everything blows over eventually. Even big explosions settle down after a few weeks and months.

the breakup survival guide

There's no doubt about it. Breakups suck. And lesbian breakups are the worst because we live in small, insular communities and hang out at all the same coffee shops, bars, restaurants, and bookstores. You will see your ex wherever you go. For weeks you will run into friends who ask where so-and-so is. People will gossip and talk about your breakup. Friends will take sides. What was once communal space will feel dangerous if not downright hostile. But with the right tools you'll get through it and come out stronger, hotter, and smarter.

There's no such thing as a happy breakup, even if you were the one who wanted out of the relationship. It's an abrupt change to your routine and it means doing things alone, like eating and sleeping, that you usually did with someone else. But if you've ended a relationship, there's a reason for it. You weren't getting along or you weren't good for each other in some way. And now it's time to move on. Read through this section and use the parts that feel comfortable. Each of us reacts differently to a breakup.

are you really broken up?

First assess the situation. Often a breakup was simply a hysterical reaction to feeling threatened. Breakups are one of those emotional tools people use for leverage, and sometimes they get thrown around when they shouldn't. I'm not saying this is healthy. It's not. And if this kind of thing is going on in your relationship, you should probably address it. But sometimes a little bit of space, some clear thinking, and maybe some counseling are all you need to fix something that seems permanently broken.

People in couples may try to manipulate each other by threatening to break up. Breakups happen when people are upset and don't know what else to do. Is this a breakup in name only? When one or both of you calms down or sobers up, are you going to start screaming for your baby to come home from the neighbors' like Stanley Kowalski? If it's that type of breakup, you won't need this survival guide. All you need to do is take a break, get a good night's sleep, and call her up to process the next day.

stick a fork in me, i'm done

If you are still reading, then this must be a real breakup. One that you want to stick. And I'm going to tell you how to make it stick.

Do not call the person you are breaking up with. Under any circumstances. I don't care how badly you want to talk or how lonely you are. What you need more than anything is clarity and the mental space to figure things out outside of your partner's presence. Take a deep breath and put the phone down.

the first three days

The first 72 hours are the worst. This is the danger zone. It's the relapse period—the part of the breakup when the additive feelings are still working and seem stronger than reason and logic. So for the first 72 hours, set yourself up with some type of support structure. Go to a friend's house. Arrange to sleep on his or her couch for a few days if possible. Try not to be alone because that's when you're emotional.

Read theory. Reading theory about love and breakups can help you intellectualize the process and sometimes that can help take some of the pain out of it. Read theory about sex and relationships, about love, read self-help books. Just give it a try. If these topics really turn you off, try reading romances. Allow yourself to get sad and cry. Let it drain you.

OK, so you've stockpiled your theory and self-help, or your romance or other juicy fiction. You are going to need some supplies so you are pretty well taken care of for the first 72 hours. And grocery shopping will help occupy your mind.

Do you have vices? Well, now is not the time to quit. Go buy yourself a small amount of whatever your favorite vice is:

chocolate, cigarettes, whiskey, porn. Whatever you need, have a moderate amount on hand—provided it's not heroin or guns and it doesn't reignite an addiction or conflict with a medication—it's OK to indulge right now. I'm not condoning binge behavior: If you wake up and your underwear is hanging off the ceiling fan and there's a stranger next to you asking what's for breakfast, you've probably gone overboard.

Buy food. You're upset, and low blood sugar will only aggravate the way you feel and make you less stable. Buy yourself simple healthy meals. If you cook, buy chicken breasts, sweet potatoes, green vegetables, a good loaf of French bread and maybe splurge on a bottle of good wine. If you don't cook, put together a no-cook snack plate with radishes and cumbers, cold cuts, cheese, and crackers.

Stay far away from all forms of communication. Don't log in to instant messenger. Don't look at her Friendster page or Myspace page to see if she has changed her relationship status yet. Don't reread old text messages or e-mails. Just let it go. Give yourself time to let your emotional response dull a bit.

the next few weeks

When you feel ready, call friends and make dates. Throw movie nights. Occupy yourself with social events. Ask your friends not to talk to you about the goings on in your ex's life. Relearn what it's like to do things on your own.

Try reconnecting with friends you may have neglected while you were busy in a relationship. Remind yourself how functional and happy you were before your relationship. You were fine before, you will be fine again.

Don't be afraid to seek help if you need it. Talking to friends is fine, but if it's really difficult to let go of anger or hurt, it may be time to talk to a professional. Therapy can help get you back on track.

for maximum drama

For Maximum Drama, or FMD, is a reference to making the worst possible choice in any given situation. If the best way to deflate a possible situation is to walk away and you choose to stay and engage, you have made the FMD choice. Other examples of FMD situations include: cheating, sleeping with friends of your lover, sleeping with friends, lying, being emotionally irresponsible. Try and avoid this kind of activity.

payback's a bitch

Sometimes we're emotionally healthy and sometimes we're childish brats. We don't have to be grown up one hundred percent of the time. If you really can't resist acting out and no amount of therapy or yoga seems to be helping, go ahead and give in. Just make sure you don't do anything that's really harmful! And don't tell anyone I told you it was OK.

Not that I'm condoning this in any way, but there are sites online that allow you to send an anonymous e-card to former lovers telling them they might have picked up a little something and should maybe head to the clinic.

Just last week I got a phone call from a woman I used to be involved with. She said that her new girlfriend had found one of my earrings. She went on and on about New Girl sleeping on "the side of the bed that you used to sleep on," and it was a very painful, emotionally draining conversation. After I got off the phone, I took a few deep breaths, drank some chamomile tea, and then sat down at my laptop and anonymously informed her that she might have scabies.

the revenge-sex phenomena

Revenge sex is pretty self-explanatory. It's a bad choice but seems to be a common one. Revenge sex is when you sleep with someone in order to get back at someone who has hurt you. Really, what's a more effective way to upset your ex than sleeping with her brother?

Sometimes bad choices seem calculated when they are in fact nothing more than poor impulse control. Revenge sex has to be intentional in order to count. I had an ex accuse me of revenge sex once. After we broke up, I did what any heartbroken, emotionally unstable butch-loving high femme would do. I got drunk and slept with another butch in town who she knew.

In reality I was simply lonely and looking for solace—and I wanted to get laid, of course. But that simple act of neediness sent such powerful shockwaves through my circle of acquaintances that I ended up facing eighteen months of ostracism. My ex's friends—and there were a lot of them—picked sides (hers, of course). I couldn't go to a lesbian bar, event, club, or coffee shop without encountering some scandalized dyke glaring at me with a roving horse eye.

"They play on the same football team, and they have to look at each other every Sunday," one concerned party explained. I'd apparently crossed a line that should never be crossed: sleeping with two butches on the same football team. I'm sure the parties involved would be happy to know that the suffering I endured outweighed the hot sex I got. Had I actually wanted to enact some sort of revenge, this situation would have been great. It was certainly effective. They hate each other to this day.

fucking up friendships

Another way dykes act out is by splitting up friendships by inserting themselves between two friends. "I've totally fucked people to get revenge," explains my pal Jen, a 30-year-old

Manhattan resident. "Actually, I was dating this transguy Jeff. I was really into him. But after a few months he just stopped returning my calls. No processing, nothing. I never even knew what went wrong. But while I was calling and not getting called back, I made friends with his roommate, who often answered the phone.

"The roommate's name was Ian, and I think she felt kind of sorry for me. One day she asked if I wanted to go out for coffee, and I accepted. So to get back at Jeff, I seduced Ian and began sleeping with her. It was great because I'd spend the night all the time and Jeff would have to see me in the mornings. I made sure to walk around naked a lot."

I asked Jen how she really felt about Ian. "I liked her, and I was attracted to her, but I wasn't into her the way I was into Jeff," she answered. "I just really liked the idea that Jeff had to see me all the time. I liked that he had to listen to us having sex. It was really the thought of getting back at Jeff that made the sex so hot."

Jen fucked Ian just long enough to ruin the friendship she had with Jeff. A few months after the two of them hooked up, the relationship between Jeff and Ian became so strained that Jeff moved out and Ian was forced to get another roommate.

"Once Jeff was gone, my interest in Ian started to wane, and eventually we broke it off. I just wasn't that into fucking him without the Jeff part."

the dyke and the bi girl: a love triangle

Karen, a 29-year-old former San Franciscan who now lives in Brooklyn, was involved in a cycle of sex for revenge in college. "I was sleeping with a woman named Kate, and she was also sleeping with Adam. Adam was in love with me, and I think he was sleeping with Kate as a way to get to me," she says. "Kate hated men. She'd had mostly terrible relationships with them and decided she'd only date women. It was problematic for her, though, because I don't really believe she was attracted to women. I think she was sleeping with me out of a very real desire to reject men, but I never felt like that translated into a desire for me."

Kate's desire to punish an entire gender through sex was apparently effective. Karen goes on to explain that Kate's behavior made Adam feel demoralized and inadequate. He often stated that he felt as if he could never make either of them happy in the long term because he wasn't female.

"She was sleeping with both of us, and this hurt Adam. He felt like she was constantly saying he wasn't enough for her. She was punishing him, and through him all men," explains Karen.

"Kate continued to sleep with Adam as revenge because I was growing disinterested in her. I had become bored and irritated, and would get really high and fall asleep so I wouldn't have to fuck her. Finally, I slept with Adam myself, knowing that he was in love with me and knowing that it would hurt him. It seemed the easiest way to get rid of Kate. After we slept together, Adam and Kate went back to fucking. I think she fucked him to punish him for ruining her relationship with me."

"i'm getting laid now, by the way"

The sex-for-revenge scenario doesn't always include a set of friends, or a three-way love affair. Rachel, a 24-year-old San Francisco film student, had sex to get the attention of her ambivalent nonmonogamous girlfriend. Hoping that proving she was desirable to other girls would encourage her girlfriend to be more serious about their relationship, she hooked up with one of her coworkers.

"I went out dancing with a girl from work, and ended up sleeping with her," she explains. "It worked, sort of. Tara got really pissed off at me and has been more possessive and coupley. But she also doesn't trust me now. It's a fucked situation because we had never agreed to be a monogamous couple, but it was just sort of assumed. It's not like she was sleeping with anyone else—she just always treated me in a way that seemed blasé. I got her attention this time. I hope she gets over the whole thing pretty soon. I'm sick of apologizing."

Simply getting some action in front of your former lover is another way to go about it. Kelly, a 32-year-old waitress, was so hurt by her girlfriend's departure that she took to frequenting the same bars as her ex and actively flaunting her ability to get attention from women.

"It started out as an accident," she explains. "I actually made out with a woman in front of her because I was drunk and didn't really realize she was watching me. She got really angry and yelled at me about how I couldn't just show up at a club and pick up whatever trash was lying around. Once I realized how much it pissed her off, I started doing it on purpose. She left me, but there's no way I'm going to let her think that I'm sitting around waiting for her to call me and apologize."

why girls go there

"You have to be pretty shut off from your emotions to not care that your girlfriend is with someone else. I really think it's something we've all done whether we readily admit it or not," says M. J., a 31-year-old filmmaker.

Adding that she believes revenge sex commonly goes by other labels, M. J. explains, "Well, I mean a lot of the time my motives are fucked up, but I don't realize it until later. I think half the women I've slept with have in some way been mixed-up in feelings about my first girlfriend. She really messed me up. She was a fucking bitch. She cheated on me and lied about it for months. I tried to get back at her for years by sleeping with as many girls as I could. Even when I've really been in love, there's still some kind of less-than-loving motivation. There's always some hangover from the last girl I was with."

the art of revenge sex

If you are ruminating on a bad affair and consider-
ing acting out, try quelling some of that urge with a
little movie watching instead. Both *Showgirls* and *All
About Eve* are suitable for any occasion in which revenge might be necessary, but if you want something
a little headier try *Les Biches (The Does)*, a late-six-
ties French film by Claude Chabrol. It has the perfect
combination of lesbian drama and sixties eyeliner to
distract you for a good portion of the afternoon.

One of the reasons the movie is so effective at putting a silly affair to rest is that the characters are just
way more fucked-up than you'll ever be. They move
back and forth in a tangled three-way; the two lesbian
characters bonding first, and then each of them alter-
nately attaching themselves to the male character, out
of both an attraction to him and as a way of punishing
each other for that attraction.

Frederique, an older, wealthier woman, first seduces Why, a transient artist whose emotional immaturity
is indicated by her sidewalk chalk drawings of sad-
eyed does. Frederique takes her home and cleans her
up, dresses her in nice clothes, and essentially gives
her the role of girlfriend/sex toy without offering her
much emotionally. At first Why is thrilled to have attention lavished upon her, but eventually Frederique's
coldness and emotional distance alienates her and
she begins a sexual relationship with Paul, some guy
friend of Frederique's she finds hanging around.

Frederique becomes interested in Paul after she
discovers his relationship to Why, and she seduces
him almost immediately. It's an easy task, because

Why, though very beautiful, is simple, and Paul quickly loses interest in her.

The film is driven by the subtle symmetry of the characters' movements, and their motives remain unclear even to the end. We never really understand why either of the women sleeps with Paul. It's possible that he's simply a tool to be thrown back and forth between the two women. Why sleeps with Paul as revenge for Frederique's coldness and emotional unavailability. But she also feels love for him. Frederique sleeps with Paul to get revenge for Why's infidelity, but she's also attracted to Paul and wants him. He's her equal, whereas Why is like a little girl.

Shortly after Frederique seduces Paul, there is a scene in which Why stands outside the door as they have sex. Why listens to their moans and caresses the door handle in a way that seems sexual but is also tinged with misery and desperation, and the sharp pain she experiences from being rejected by both of her love objects is clear. Eventually Paul isn't an effective enough tool for revenge and Why murders Frederique. The last scene in the film is haunting, because Why has not only killed Frederique but taken her place as Paul's lover, wearing her clothes and perfume and copying her mannerisms. It's never clear if she kills the love object who betrayed her or the rival who has stolen her love object away.

sex with the ex

Sleeping with your ex, rather than simply sleeping with his or her best friend, is another form of revenge sex. While the motives seem incredibly convoluted, sleeping with an ex who dumped you is all about regaining power. For instance, lingering and continuing to sleep with an ex lover after you've agreed to stop seeing each other can keep that person from moving on.

We have sex for many different reasons. And when we use sex to get revenge, we not only get back at our love object but we get to feel desirable because a new person is attracted to us. Also, tortured, romantic plotting and pining away after a loved one who has rejected you have their appeal. However, having sex for revenge is a fairly transparent way to piss someone off, which is what makes it such great fodder for subplots on *The L Word*. Just don't expect your pettiness to go unnoticed.

when the relationship isn't over

Sometimes we sleep with our exes for less nefarious reasons. Sex with an ex-girlfriend can be comforting in times of loneliness and need. Dykes create family out of ex-lovers, and an ex can provide intimacy, sex, love, and support when you most need it. Because exes are familiar with us, they understand us, and reconnecting in a sexual way can be a fulfilling experience when we need love.

surviving the worst-case scenario

SOMETIMES WE HAVE bad dates. We don't like the person we're dating: They bore us so much we want to jam a fork into our eye, they play folk music on the jukebox, they insult our friends, they text-message friends through dinner. Dates can go wrong. But don't despair. There's always a way out.

how to figure out your date's preferred pronoun

As an actively dating femme in today's multigendered society, this can be a real roadblock. The typical signs may not be applicable here, so I've broken down some last-resort methods for those in-between types.

Watch which bathroom they go in, or see if they express any anxiety about going to the bathroom (this will not work in a unisex bathroom situation or packed bar where queers take over both bathroom lineups).

Start conversation with a light ice-breaking topic like Michigan Womyn's Music Festival.

Ask the bartender.

Plan the date at your apartment, crank the heat, and see if they whip their shirt off.

Look it up on the Internet (Myspace, Friendster, etc.). Google them. You know you want to.

Straight up ask them, or look bored and wait five minutes for them to tell you their entire gender history. If it's going slow, prompt the conversation with "*Sooo*—what do you think about gender?"

how to tell if your date is a jerk

1. They're more interested in their cell phone than you.
2. They go to the bathroom when the check comes.
3. When you go anywhere with them, you get a million dirty looks from other girls.
4. The local bartender won't serve them.
5. They don't make sure you have a safe way home.
6. They can't stop talking about their ex.
7. You're at a club, it's been two hours, and they don't know where you are.

Ditching a bad date

If your date is going terribly and she's too much of a blowhard to let you explain that you don't think you are clicking, then you may be forced to ditch her.

There are several ways to do this. Use these tactics only when absolutely necessary. You can't ditch your date just because she's boring and you remembered there was a Friends rerun on.

Fake a mental illness: Start talking to yourself at dinner. Say, "Oh, I think I forgot to take my mood stabilizers." Or look around in a shocked manner. Ask her if she heard anything. If she says no, ask again. Repeat as needed.

Fake an emergency: Give your cell phone number to a friend and ask her to call you at an appointed hour that falls somewhere during dinner. If dinner is going well, ignore the call, your date will feel special. If dinner is a drag, take the call, begin sobbing, and explain that a family member, a cherished pet, or a favorite celebrity has died and you need to go home immediately.

Go to the bathroom and never come back: Pick up your handbag and excuse yourself to the ladies room. Call a cab on your cell phone. Check to make sure no one is watching and make a break for the parking lot.

CHAPTER 10

couples and how to be one

ARE YOU READY to be a couple? Are you experiencing the warning signs of impending coupledom? If you've found someone you really enjoy spending time with, she really enjoys spending time with you, and you find that you are spending five or six nights a week together, it's possible, just possible, that it's time to on to the next phase: girlfriends.

so, now you're girlfriends

THE FIRST THING you need to keep in mind is that there is no such thing as a relationship without problems. Once you accept that, you can figure out ways to fix the problems that will inevitably surface. According to psychotherapist Linnda Durre, author of *Great Relationships*, poor communication is the number one problem that couples face. Learning to communicate, and communicate well, can make a relationship solid and healthy.

how great relationships are made

Dr. Linnda Durre has written a manual of over 200 pages of questions for couples to ask each other. The questions in the book cover the minutiae of a couple's daily life, right down to the simplest, most unimportant-seeming preferences. If you want to make a serious effort to get to know your partner, this manual can really help you lay down some groundwork. I called Dr. Durre to find out some ways that learning how to talk—and really get to know—the person you are in a relationship with can help the two of you be happy.

What do you see as the biggest relationship saboteurs for dyke couples?

DR. DURRE: Infidelity is the biggest one. And holding things in is another. Couples are afraid that if they talk, they will break up. Many people don't take time to look inside themselves, and then do the same thing to their mate. They expect their mate to be psychic and read their mind, which is impossible and unfair. I've seen couples who have been together for years but don't know some of the simplest things about each other. It always astounds me. But resolving issues, especially when done correctly with a therapist, makes couples closer. They feel like war buddies.

But what about white lies and simply being polite?

DR. DURRE: There's a difference between politeness and caring about someone and being diplomatic. Couples need to learn diplomacy. Most people don't know how to listen. Most people don't know how to affirm other people's perceptions when they disagree.

Does disagreeing on basic preferences mean a couple is doomed?

DR. DURRE: Some people can live with more disagreements and incompatibility than others. It depends on the couple. There are ways to compromise and collaborate so everyone can win.

Give and take is part of a good relationship. If there are intolerable differences like basic values, spiritual/religious beliefs, or wanting a child, then either they have to agree to disagree or separate.

How should couples use the *Great Relationships* manual?

DR. DURRE: Make an appointment with each other. Turn off the cell phones, TV, extraneous noise, and go through the book. Fill out all the pages, then give your book to your mate, read the whole thing, and make notes about what you'd like to discuss. Many people are surprised at all the new things they learn about their partner. Sometimes they feel duped, like they've been playing a game and not knowing the rules.

What about mystery? Doesn't that make relationships more exciting?

DR. DURRE: If mystery means keeping someone guessing or driving them insane by not communicating about their needs, mystery should be redefined as "crazy making," which usually leads to fights. If someone wants mystery, read Nancy Drew.

How important do you see things like sex and desire in a long-term relationship?

DR. DURRE: Very important. You have to have a spark, and it's important to desire that person sexually. Many times when the sex drive has died down, friendship remains and that's equally important. Some couples really don't care that much about sex as they age and they realize that the friendship, closeness, comfort, and emotional intimacy are more important. You have the right to be picky when looking for a partner. Put yourself in a place where you will be exposed to people who share your interests. Sometimes it's easier to write things down than to say them to your partner, so my manual is a first step for those who have difficulty talking. My book is to empower people to have loving, close, intimate, relationships so they can have hot, fun sex and live happy lives!

spend time apart

It's not uncommon to start spending all your free time together in the beginning of a relationship. We get so caught up in each other's presence—just talking, getting to know someone, having sex, and basking in being together—that we lose sight of our outside lives. Suddenly the laundry is piling up, the cat is wasting away, you've missed the last several episodes of *Project Runway*, and your refrigerator is full of rotting tofu.

Take some space. She may want some time with her friends but not know how to bring it up. Or you may need some time away but instead stay with her every night out of fear of losing her. Let her know how much you like her. Continually reassure her and yourself. Check in with each other and try paying attention to what is going on in your life outside the relationship.

our relationships are different

We create our own relationships. They don't have to look like anyone else's. There is no right way or wrong way to be a couple. Spend as much time together or apart as you feel you need. Don't compare yourselves to other couples. Do what's right for you.

20 red flags

Red flags come in all forms. For you a red flag might be that your partner doesn't like sushi. But there are some red flags that indicate serious problems. If you find yourself experiencing any of these situations, you should seriously think about getting the hell out of the relationship you are in.

1. You are being physically abused.
2. You are being emotionally abused.
3. Your partner criticizes you incessantly.
4. Your partner doesn't like you to have friends outside of your relationship.
5. You are never able to spend time alone with friends or family.
6. Your friends and family seem concerned about the health of your relationship.
7. Your partner frequently drinks to excess.
8. Your partner uses drugs more often than your are comfortable with
9. Your partner makes you feel unsafe.
10. You are constantly under threat of being broken up with.
11. Your partner lies to you.
12. Your partner disappears for long periods of time and doesn't account for her whereabouts.
13. Your partner coerces you into sex.
14. Your partner withholds sex.
15. Your partner punishes you by being emotionally withdrawn when you do something she doesn't like.

16. Your partner insists on paying for everything and you feel dependent on this.
17. Your partner refuses to pay for anything
18. Your partner has a problem with compulsive behavior, such as gambling or porn.
19. Your partner embarrasses you in front of your friends.
20. Your partner frequently makes scenes in public.

moving into long-term territory

Is she the love of your life? How do you know? Is there such a thing? The way we talk about love affects the way we experience it. When we use terms like "the one," it can confuse us. It's different for every person. It's important to remember to take things day by day, continually assess and stop looking for your love to look like something from the movies.

Long-term doesn't have to mean forever. Long-term can mean several months or years. Don't freak yourself out about it before you get there.

The important thing is that you have a good time and learn more about yourself. Now get out there and find that lady!

ACKNOWLEDGEMENTS

THANKS TO EVERYONE who put up with me while I was writing this book. I would never have gotten anywhere without Shannon Berning as my editor, so first and foremost I have to thank her. She's beyond patient, even when I am a bit on the spastic side. She makes my writing better and gets my sense of humor even when it's twisted.

Thanks to my dear friend Jess who answered my questions and talked to me about sex when I needed perspective. Thanks to Grace Moon for lots of smart conversation and having a vision. Thanks to all the girls I met all over the country who talked to me about their personal lives. Thanks to all the women at Mich Fest who gave me their pick up lines and told me their dating stories. Thanks to Kate for distracting me in a good way and keeping me out of my head enough to write about dating even while I was doing it.

ABOUT THE AUTHOR

DIANA CAGE'S previous books include *The On Our Backs Guide to Lesbian Sex*, *Box Lunch*, *Threeways*, and several erotica anthologies. She has written about sex and dating for a variety of publications including *Girlfriends*, *Curve*, and *Frontiers*, and given sex advice in *Maxim* and *GQ*. She is the managing editor of *Velvetpark* magazine and the former editor of the lesbian sex magazine, *On Our Backs*.